Intermittent Fasting & Keto Diet

The Rapid Weight Loss Combination

By: Sebastian Beach

Table of Contents

Intermittent Fasting

Wear Your Favorite Pair of Jeans, Look Good In Photos and Feel Sexy Again!

Introduction

The journey to weight loss can often seem long and daunting. Whether you are cutting out foods you enjoy, counting calories, or starting to incorporate exercise into your life, it is not very hard to get discouraged when you're not seeing the results you want in the time you expected to see them. Often times, dieting and exercising feel like chores, and the stress they add to your life nearly counteracts their healthy effects. With intermittent fasting, weight loss no longer has to feel like a burden. Intermittent fasting is a method of dieting that focuses on eating patterns rather than food choice entirely.

Intermittent fasting allows you to still eat the foods you love while still being able to lose weight and gain muscle mass. Intermittent fasting is a method utilized by many bodybuilders, athletes, and fitness gurus to achieve perfect physique. The method follows the science of the body and can be practiced short term or long term. There are numerous approached to intermittent fasting, so it is easy to find a path that best suits you and your lifestyle.

This book will detail the science of intermittent fasting, describe why it works, teach you about the differences between proteins, carbs, and explain the role calories play in the world of nutrition. This book will show you exactly how you can stop depriving yourself, say "Yes!" to your cravings, and learn to enjoy a healthier lifestyle as you achieve your weight loss goals more rapidly than you would with a typical exercise programs or dieting alone. This book will also detail numerous food plans to help you get started, as well expel perpetuated eating and nutrition myths that could be hurting, rather than helping you achieve your goals.

This book is meant to educate and motivate. Intermittent fasting takes the guess work out of dieting and gives you a clear-cut path to a healthier you. Don't give up on your fitness journey until you have tried this method. With intermittent fasting, you will find you are more than capable of living a healthy, happy lifestyle that you truly enjoy!

Chapter 1: What is Intermittent Fasting?

When it comes to working out and trying to lose weight, there is not shortage to the types of diet plans that are out there for you to try. You may be amazed at how many workout plans and diet plans that you can choose from and even though they are all going to have different information, often conflicting information, you will find that they all promise to be the best and safest way for you to lose the weight.

In reality, most of these are not going to be safe for your body at all. They often leave out the important nutrition that you need to stay safe and healthy in the hopes that you will eat fewer calories and lose weight. And while this can work for the short term, if you go on the diet for the long term (something that isn't that likely since they are so hard to stick to and you often gain all the weight back), you could suffer a lot of bad health issues.

When it comes time to start losing weight and getting your health back, intermittent fasting could be the method that you will find successful. The common misconception with this option is that you are losing weight because you are starving yourself. This may seem like what is going on when you see someone is fasting, but in reality, it is not a limit to how much you can eat, rather it is more of a limit on the times of day that you can eat.

With intermittent fasting, you are choosing to fast and then feast, but with a purpose. During the feast parts, you are going to eat all of your calories and nutrition during specified periods of the day, rather than letting it spread out through the whole day. This is often more effective because you can train your mind to only eat during certain parts of the day, rather than letting yourself graze whenever you wanted. Plus, you will eat fewer calories during that time of the day compared to eating all throughout the day, while still feeling full and satisfied.

Of course, there are a few ways that you will be able to participate in intermittent fasting, and we will discuss some of the different options in the chapters to follow, but the idea is to limit the amount of time that you are allowed to eat during the day. You may limit yourself to just one meal a day, have a few days a week when you won't eat at all (or limit your calories to under 500), or even picking a small amount of time, usually 8 hours or less, where you are allowed to eat, and the rest of the time you are on a fast.

One of the main benefits of this is that you are going to eat less than you were on any other diet. Since you are not allowed to eat all day long, you will avoid grazing and eating more calories than planned. In addition, when you have to fit all of your calories and nutrition into just a few short hours, you are going to fill u pretty quickly and are less likely to eat as many calories as you would if you ate your traditional times.

But this is only a part of the story as you will find out. Not only are you cutting out the calories, but you are also timing your meals so that your body will react in a certain way, making it easier to burn more calories. The process of fasting is going to make it easier for the body to burn through those calories in a more efficient manner, helping you to not only eat a lower amount of calories overall but also helping the body create a deficit of calories because you are using up more than before.

This may seem counterintuitive. Most people assume that when they go on a fast, they are not only depleting their bodies of some of the nutrients it needs, but they are also putting the body into starvation mode, making it lose fewer calories and making it even harder to lose the weight. While it is true that the body can go into starvation mode if you fast too long, there is a small time frame where the body can go without food, and it will actually speed up the metabolism for a short period of time.

The intermittent fasting diet is going to use these times of sped up metabolism to its advantage. You are not going to fast for so long in between meals that you start to go into starvation mode; you are going to fast for just long enough to get the full benefits of that faster metabolism before you go ahead and eat again. The trick here is to plan out the meals that you will enjoy and make sure that you are eating at the right times to burn the calories and still avoid the issues with going into starvation mode.

Another trick here is to make sure that you are still getting the nutrition that you want. Even though you are limiting the amount of time that you are allowed to eat, you need to make sure that you are getting the right amount of calories in each day. While a little deficit is good, you should not get so low that you aren't going to be able to fuel the body. Learn how many calories you should have for your body and your activity level, and try to stay pretty close to this number each day, even with the limited time for eating. This will ensure that the body is not going to start dragging and missing out and will keep it out of starvation mode.

In addition to eating enough calories, you should make sure that you are getting the right types of nutrition. While you don't have to carefully count calories on this diet, you are not allowed to go out there and eat as much sugar and chocolate as you want. You need to eat a balanced diet that has many fruits, vegetables, lean meats and more to keep the body running smoothly, to help keep that metabolism up and running as much as possible, and to ensure that you are getting the right nutrition.

When you are able to bring all these parts together to work well, you are going to see that there is a lot of good that can come to your body. The body will still get the nutrition and calories that it needs, and you are going to be surprised that you can feel full and satisfied without having to eat all of the time. When you aren't concentrating on food all the time, you can free up the mind to work on other things, and you can learn to just eat in response to hunger from the body rather than as a response to the time on the clock. You are going to feel full and satisfied on this diet plan as well, even though you are cutting into some of the eating time that you may have been used to in the past. With a bit of practice, you will find that it is easier to get on the new schedule and not have to worry about when it is time to eat all the time.

Another thing that you need to keep track of when you are on the intermittent fasting diet is that you will need to do some working out as well to ensure that the metabolism is gong to keep up and running. A good combination of cardio and weight lifting is best to keep you in shape, but mixing things up can really help.

The timing of your workouts is going to make a big difference in how this diet works as well. While getting exercise into your daily routine is the most important step, and you should fit it in whenever it works the best for you, many experts agree that doing the workout during your fasting period is the best. This can ensure that the metabolism keeps going nice and strong and can be the most effective time to get the exercise in and to see those calories go faster than ever.

As you can see, the idea of intermittent fasting is a pretty simple one, one that does not have to be that difficult to follow as long as you make some adjustments to your eating schedule and you know how to stay disciplined enough to not eat all throughout the day. There may be times when you have some issues and will need additional help to make this all work for you, but over time, you will see that the intermittent fasting diet is one of the easiest, as well as one of the most effective, diets on the market for helping you to lose weight and to feel so much better about yourself.

Yes, you have probably heard about a lot of different diet plans that are out on the market. Due to the fact that many Americans are eating a diet that is unhealthy and bad for them, it is no wonder that a lot of people want to finally find the eating solution that is going to be good for them and will actually help them to lose the weight and be as healthy as possible.

The issue is that the diet industry makes millions of dollars each year. People are desperate for that get healthy quick idea and many times they will spend a lot of money in the hopes of reaching it. The biggest issue is that many of these products, as well as the diets that are promoted, are not that effective. Even if you are able to lose some weight on them, the diets and the products are unhealthy, can't be kept up with for the long term, and can even make the user really sick with continued use.

Finding a diet program like the intermittent fasting diet may seem like it is all a hoax and if you have been dealing with trying to lose weight for a long time, you may feel that this diet plan is not going to work out for you. But it is important to remember that the fasting diet is going to work a bit differently than you will find with the other diets.

The intermittent fast is not about limiting your calories all the time. It is not about buying a lot of extra products in the hopes of losing weight while taking in a lot of harmful chemicals. It is not about eating weird foods, cutting out food so much that you get sick, or some of the other questionable things that are going to be brought up with some of the other diets.

Yes, you are going to spend time limiting when you are going to eat, but this is in order to teach the body how to burn more calories and to help your metabolism to really work as well as it should. You are not limiting it so much that you never get to eat. You get to pick the calories that you want to eat during the eating time, and you are sure to get as many calories, and perhaps even more than you need to keep the body functioning. There are even suggestions on how to eat the right foods to feel good and get nutrition and lots of guides on how to exercise. This diet plan puts in a lot of the good stuff that you would need inside a healthy diet plan and ensure that you get everything that you need to stay healthy while also losing weight.

The intermittent diet is going to take some time to learn how to use, and it may be difficult to start in the beginner (we aren't used to having to limit the amount of time that we are allowed to eat during the day), but with a bit of practice and learning how to eat the right kinds of foods at the right times of the day, you will find that getting in the best health of your life doesn't have to be as complicated as you would think. Try out one of the intermittent fast options in the following chapter and see how easy this kind of diet plan can be.

Chapter 2: Why It Works

Intermittent fasting is the practice of scheduling your meals in order for your body to get the most out of them. Rather than cutting your calorie intake in half, depriving yourself of all the foods you enjoy, or diving into a trendy diet fad, intermittent fasting is a simple, logical, and healthful way of eating that promotes fat loss. There are many ways to approach intermittent fasting, but it's most basically defined as a specific eating pattern. This method focuses on changing when you eat, rather than what you eat.

When you begin intermittent fasting, you will most likely keep your calorie intake the same, but rather than spreading your meals throughout the day, you will eat bigger meals during a shorter time frame. For example, rather than eating 3 to 4 meals a day, you might eat one large meal at 11am, then another large meal at 6pm, with no meals in between 11am and 6pm, and after 6pm, no meals until 11am the next day. This is only one method of intermittent fasting, and others will be detailed in this book in later chapters, but first you must understand why this method works.

Intermittent fasting is a method utilized by many bodybuilders, athletes, and fitness gurus to keep their muscle mass high and their body fat percentage low. It is a simple strategy that allows you to eat the foods you enjoy, while still promoting fat loss and muscle gain or maintenance. Intermittent fasting can be practiced short term or long term, but the best results come from implanting this method into your daily lifestyle.

Though the word "fasting" may make alarm the average person, intermittent fasting does not equate to starving yourself. To understand the principals behind successful intermittent fasting, we'll first go over the two body's two states digestion, the fed state, and the fasting state. For three to five hours after eating a meal, your body is in what is known as the "fed state." During the fed state, your insulin levels increase in order to absorb and digest your food. When your insulin levels are high, it is very difficult for your body to burn fat. Insulin is a hormone produced by the pancreas in order to regulate glucose levels in the bloodstream. Though its purpose is to regulate, insulin is technically a storage hormone. When insulin levels are high, your body is burning your food for energy, rather than your stored fat which is why increased levels of it prevent weight loss.

After the three to five hours are up, your body has finished processing the meal, and you enter the post-absorptive state. The post-absorptive state lasts anywhere from 8 to 12 hours. After this time gap is when your body enters the fasted state. Since your body has completely processed your food by this point, your insulin levels are low, making your stored fat extremely accessible for burning. In the fasted state, your body has no food left to utilized for energy, so your stored fat is burned instead. Intermittent fasting allows your body to reach an advanced fat burning state that you would normally reach with the average, 'three meals per day' eating pattern. This factor alone is the reason why many people notice rapid results with intermittent fasting without even making changes to their exercise routines, how much they eat, or what they eat. They are simply changing the timing and pattern of their food intake.

When you begin an intermittent fasting program, it may take some time to get into the swing of things. Don't get discouraged! If you slip up, just get back into your intermittent fasting pattern when you can. Avoid beating yourself up, or feeling guilty. Negative self-talk will only prolong you getting back to your pattern. Making a lifestyle change takes a conscience effort, and no expects you to do it perfectly right away. If you are not used to going long periods without eating, intermittent fasting will take some getting used to. As long as you choose the right method for you, stay focused and remain positive, you will get the hang of it in no time.

Unlike some of the other diet plans that you may go on, the intermittent fast is one that is going to work. It uses your body and how it works to its advantage to help you to really lose weight. It is easy to get a bit scared when you hear about fasting. You may assume that you are going to have to spend days and weeks without eating (and who really has the willpower to give up their food for that long even when they do want to lose weight), and that it is going to be too hard for you.

Intermittent fasting is a bit different than you may imagine. Not only is it really hard to go on a fast for weeks at a time, but it is also not good for the whole body. Your body will often go into starvation mode if you end up being on the fast for too long. It assumes that you are in a time without much food and so the body will work on saving the calories and helping you to hold on to the fat and calories for as long as you possibly can. This means that not only are you hungry, but you are also missing out on losing the weight that you want.

You don't have to get too worried about how this intermittent fast is going to work with the starvation mode. The intermittent fast is going to be so effective because it isn't going to let you fast for so long that the body goes into this starvation mode and you stop losing calories and weight. Instead, it is going to make the fast last just long enough that you will actually be able to speed up the metabolism a bit.

With the intermittent fast, you will find that when you go for a few hours without eating, usually no more than 24ish hours at a time, the body is not going to go right into the starvation mode. Rather, it is actually going to speed up through some of the calories that are inside. If you ate the right amount of calories for the day, the body is then going to revert to eating up the stored reserves of fat in the body to help fuel it along. So with this kind of fast, you are avoiding starvation mode and rather turning your body into a machine that is able to eat through more calories than usual without you having to put in more work!

If you are able to pick out the right kind of intermittent fast that you want to follow, stick to it for the long term, and ensure that the foods that you do eat in between your fast are lower in calories, full of healthy nutrition, and good for you, you are going to be pretty amazed at the results that you get from the intermittent fast. Make sure to add in some good weight lifting and cardio exercising, and you will get the results that you want in no time.

Some tips for going on the intermittent fast

When you are getting started on a new diet plan, it is important to get a few tips that is going to make it a bit easier for you to accomplish. Sometimes a new diet plan is going to be a bit harder to work on because it is different compared to some of the habits that you had before. Some of the tips that you are able to follow when it comes time to working with intermittent fasting to ensure that you are going to see the best results include:

- Take things slowly—changing up the eating habits that you have can be tough. You will need to find the method that is right for you, and if you need to start out with just a few days on the fast and the rest as regular days and slowly build up to doing this all of the time, that is fine. If you rush yourself too much, you are more likely to fail in the long run. This can make you want to give up, and you will never see the results that you want. The best option is to go at the speed that you would like until you reach the full potential and see some of the great results.

- Don't fast for too long—the idea with intermittent fasting is to speed up the metabolism so that you are able to lose weight faster. If you end up fasting for too long, you will find that it is not going work as well. If you fast for too long and restrict the calories too much, the body is going to go into starvation mode in order to try and keep you alive for longer, effectively burning fewer calories overall. The methods behind the intermittent fasting is meant to help you to fast for just long enough to speed the metabolism but not so long that you will stop burning calories. Follow the guidelines in the different forms of your fast, and you will be fine.

- Find a good workout plan—along with eating the right foods at the right times while on the intermittent fast; you also need to make sure that you are going on a good workout plan. Cardio workouts are great, but many people go on one of the intermittent fasts in order to gain some muscles and get the lean look that they want. The end of this guidebook is going to have some great beginner and some great advanced workouts that you can try for getting the lean muscle gains that you want. You can also try out some other workouts that will help you to stay motivated and see more of the results that you would like.

- Work on some meal plans—planning out your meals ahead of time can make the intermittent fast easier to follow. This will help you to have food and snacks on hand that are allowed within the diet parameters that you set (some of the choices will not have any restrictions on the calories, and some will restrict calories on certain days so you can plan around these). You can plan ahead by a week and make the foods on one of the days that you are free. Then throughout the week everything is going to be prepared and ready for you, saving time in the week and ensuring that you don't slip up because you weren't prepared.

- Plan ahead for fasting days—if you pick one of the plans that has a full fasting day (either one that is completely devoid of food or one that severely restricts the calories for the day), it is important to plan ahead. Make that one a busy day, one where you barely have time to eat anyway. Make the right meals ahead of time so that you aren't trying to come up with something when you are hungry and then going over your amounts. With the right preparation and choosing the right days of the week for the fast, you will see how easy this fast can be.

- Pick the type that you like—as you will see in one of the following chapters, there are many different types of intermittent fasts that you can do. they are going to vary on the amount of hours that you go in between eating, whether or not you take full days off, how many calories you can eat during the fasting and more. You will be the one who decides which fast is right for you. Take a look through each of them and see which one is going to work best for your schedule as well as for your level of commitment or issues with staying on track. All of them can provide the same great benefits; just some are easier for people to do than others.

- Find someone to do it with you: sometimes getting started on a new diet plan is hard. You want to go back to some of your old habits or some of the foods that you used to love, and it is just hard. One of the best ways that you are able to stay on a new diet plan is to find someone else to do it with you. It is best to go with someone else who will use the intermittent fast with you, but anyone who is on a diet or trying to reach one of their own goals will work well too. This is someone you can encourage and who will encourage you, someone to talk things through, and someone to bounce ideas off of so that the diet plan is easier than doing it alone.

It is normal to have some resistance with a new diet plan. You want to be able to just see the weight come off without making any changes to the way that you behave during the day. But if you try out some of the tips above, you will find that following the intermittent fast, or any other healthy diet, does not have to be as difficult as you first thought.

Chapter 3: The Difference Between Proteins, Carbohydrates, And Fats

There are three main types of nutrients our body absorbs for energy; proteins, carbohydrates, and fats. Proteins, carbohydrates, and fats are referred to as "macronutrients" and provide all the fuel our bodies need to survive. Each macronutrient nourishes the body in its own specific way, and our digestive system processes each one differently. A protein packed meal will process much differently one that is high in carbohydrates or fats. Proteins, carbohydrates, and fats come in many different forms, and not all of them are created equally. There are good and bad choices of each category of macronutrients.

Carbohydrates are the body's main source of fuel and energy. By definition, they are the sugars, starches, and fibers found in grains, fruits, vegetables and milk products. Carbohydrates provide the necessary fuel for the proper operation of multiple body functions. The central nervous system and brain functions are powered by carbohydrates. Working muscles, mood, and memory functions are also influenced by carbohydrate intake. Carbohydrates prevent the body from using protein as its energy source, thus enabling fat metabolism.

In recent years, many dieting fads have pushed participants to cut carbohydrates completely out of their diets, but this is not beneficial to the body, necessary for weight loss, or safe for your health. The fact is, there are two different types of carbohydrates. Simple and complex. The difference between them is their chemical structure which affects their rate of absorption into the body. A simple carbohydrate can be more easily digested, as it is made of just one or two sugars, while a complex carbohydrate is composed of three or more sugars. There are also "good" and "bad" carbohydrates. While the difference between simple and complex carbohydrates is based on science, the difference between good and bad carbohydrates is based on common sense nutrition. Carbs that are devoid of refined sugars and grains, low to moderate in calories, high in fiber or nutritional value, and low in sodium and saturated fat are considered good, while carbs that are full of processed sugars, high in calories, low in fiber and high in saturated fats are considered bad.

Examples of good carbs are:

- Sweet potatoes

- Legumes

- Cottage Cheese

- Bananas

- Whole Grains

- Peas

Examples of bad carbs are:

- Pizza Crust

- Bagels

- Potato Chips

- Cake

- Cookies

- Soda

Picking out the right kinds of carbs to eat will make a big difference in your overall health. It is going to help you to get the energy that you need rather than just eating a lot of bad foods, like the baked goods and those with sugars inside of them. And this is where the low carb diets get it all wrong. They assume that all carbs are the same, making you miss out on some of the good nutrition that you really need.

You need to understand how all the carbs are going to be different. In the group of bad carbs, you are taking in carbs that are basically going to be transferred into sugars inside of the body. You might as well eat a whole thing of sugar when you take in processed grains like breads and sodas because they don't have any of the nutritional value that you need. This is why when you eat a lot of sugars and a lot of processed carbs, you are increasing your risk of diabetes because you are adding so many bad sugars into the body.

On the other hand, you will also see that eating complex carbs can be good for your body. Your body does need to have some carbs inside to help it to stay healthy and strong and to give you the energy that is needed. These complex carbs are going to give you the added energy that you need while offering some of the extra nutrition that you need to stay healthy as possible. Make sure to get some of the good carbs that are listed above into your diet each day and see how it can benefit your whole life!

Protein is the next vital macronutrient on our list. Proteins are made up of amino acids, which many refer to as the "building blocks" of a healthy body. There is a total of twenty amino acids that our bodies require to function properly. Each of these amino acids is essential to us, as our organs, skin, muscles, hair and nails are all composed of protein. Protein is also responsible for the proper function of our hormones, immune system, digestive tract, and blood flow, but the human body only produces eleven out of the twenty necessary amino acids on its own. The other nine amino acids must be gained through the foods we eat, making protein an incredibly vital factor in any human being's diet.

The essential proteins that our body is incapable of creating itself are Tryptophan, Threonine, Isoleucine, Leucine, Lysine, Methionine, Phenylalanine, Valine and Histidine. When consumed, the body breaks down proteins, extracting the amino acids it needs from each food source. By definition, protein is any class of nitrogenous organic compounds that consist of large molecules composed of one or more amino acids, but just like carbohydrates, not all proteins are created equally. The protein available in an egg white is not the same as the protein provided by a piece of chicken. This is why adding variety to the protein filled food you consume is necessary. While poultry and fish contain proteins such as myosin and collagen, beans and legumes contain proteins like avidin and ovalbumin, among others. There are many different variations of proteins out there, and they are all made of amino acids. Changing up the types of proteins you consume, assures you are getting all nine essential amino acids in your diet.

Lacking the right amounts and types of proteins in your diet is detrimental to fat loss and muscle gain. When the body is low on protein, it is forced to break down the protein that is within the body to create the nine essential amino acids. This will most typically lead a decline in lean muscle mass. The muscle tissue in our bodies naturally burns fat, even when we are at rest. With absolutely no exercise, ten pounds of muscle will burn fifty calories in a day, while ten pounds of fat will only burn twenty calories. We will better explain the role of calories in your diet later on, but it easy to see why a decline in muscle mass is not in your favor.

Much like carbohydrates, there are two types of proteins; complete and incomplete. Complete proteins contain all nine essential amino acids and typically come from animal sources. Incomplete proteins are missing one or more of the nine essential amino acids. Plant-based proteins are typically classified as incomplete. While it is possible to gain all nine essential amino acids through a strict vegan or vegetarian diet, it takes more researched meal planning and greater variety in food in order to maintain a healthy protein intake.

Examples of complete proteins are:

- Meats

- Fish

- Poultry

- Eggs

Examples of incomplete proteins are:

- Beans

- Lentils

- Nuts

Nuts and lentils are a good part to add to your diet, but they should not be the primary form of protein that you should be eating. Nuts are actually better known as some of the fats that you should be eating, but a handful or so of these each da is going to be plenty to help you to get the fats that you are looking for without going overboard when it comes to your fat intake.

When you are picking out the type of protein that you are going to consume, it is best to go with the ones that are lean. Fat is not a bad thing all the time, but the lean protein sources often have more of the nutrition, such as the protein, that you need to build up some of that lean muscle with your workouts. Options like turkey, chicken without the skin, and some fish can be great. Try to get fish into your diet a few times a week because not only does it provide the lean protein that you need, but the healthy b-vitamins along with the omega-3 fatty acids are so good for losing weight, helping with mind clarity, and so much more.

The third and final macronutrient we will cover is fat. Though the word alone is jarring to many people, especially those who are on the path of weight loss, fat is a beneficial and vital part of any healthy diet. Fat is a concentrated source of energy that our bodies utilize to perform daily functions. Essential dietary fats are necessary for the growth and development of cells, as well as the proper functioning of our brains and nervous systems. Fat is responsible for transporting vitamins A, D, E, and K through the bloodstream, as well as maintaining skin and tissue health. Fat cushions our vital organs, regulates body temperature, store energy and fuels our lean muscles, as discussed earlier.

The word "fat" has gained an incredibly negative reputation, one that could be easily squashed with a bit of research. Fat creates our body's natural energy reserve, and much like it's other macronutrient counterparts, there are two main types of fats; saturated fats and unsaturated fats. Understanding the difference between the two is slightly trickier with fats than it is with carbohydrates and proteins. While unsaturated fats are typically considered the healthy one of the pair, the body does require some saturated fats to function properly. The difference between the two categories comes down to molecular structure. The best way to tell the difference between a saturated and an unsaturated fat is by its state at room temperate. Saturated fat will be in a solid state at room temperate, while an unsaturated fat would be in a liquid state at room temperature.

This is because saturated fats have no gaps between molecules, and the fat is saturated by hydrogen molecules. Unsaturated fats have double bonds. Double bonds break up the chain of hydrogen molecules, allowing the fat to liquefy when it is placed at room temperature. This explains why the body is more easily able to process unsaturated fats than it is saturated fats. Saturated fats are typically found in fatty beef, chicken with skin, lamb, and pork, as well as dairy products like cream, whole milk, and ice cream. Unsaturated fats are typically found in canola oil, olive oil, fish, and nuts.

Fat is likely the most complex macronutrient because it can easily be both healthful and harmful. The general rule is that unsaturated fats are "good", while saturated fats are "bad". Choosing between "good" and "bad" fats really just takes a bit of common sense.

Examples foods that contain good, unsaturated fats are:

- Avocado

- Almonds

- Salmon

Examples of foods that contain bad, saturated fats are:

- Butter

- Cream Cheese

- Fried Foods

Eating fats does not have to be such an evil thing. Fats are actually really good for the body, you just need to pick out the ones that are actually going to help you to take care of the body. Don't focus on the ones that are bad for you, such as the ones that you would be able to find at the fast food restaurant or in the freezer section in your grocery store. As long as you are able to find the good fats that will keep you healthy, you will find that fats are critical to staying healthy and feeling great.

Proteins, carbohydrates, and fats all contain calories. A calorie is scientifically defined as a small unit of heat energy.

We use calories to fuel every single cell in our bodies. From our brain function to our nervous system, to our muscle function, our body is dependent on calories, just like a car is dependent on gasoline. Whenever we consume food, our body can either burn or store the calories we intake. Again, all three macronutrients contain calories, as do micronutrients which are the less imperative class of nutrients. The question here is, if the body requires calories to function, how can they lead to weight gain? The answer is simple. An imbalance between the calories we eat and the calories we expend is the typical cause of being overweight. When you consume an excess of calories, many of them do not get burned, which leaves your body with only one option, to store them. While lowering daily caloric intake as a weight loss method works for some, it is not always the easiest or even most effective method. With intermittent fasting, the same calories you'd normally consume will be burned more efficiently. Intermittent fasting makes it so the calories you consume are better allocated throughout the body, leading to fat loss and muscle gain.

A lot of what makes intermittent fasting so appealing is the fact that few changes need to be made in the types of foods you eat. Though we discussed good and bad macronutrients in this chapter, don't feel pressured to make "good" choices for each of your meals right away. While it always best to eat healthy, nutrient-rich foods, intermittent fasting allows you the leeway to eat the foods you love and appease your cravings. If you're not ready to change your diet immediately, simply start by following an intermittent pattern. Over time, it is likely that you'll feel motivated to make more healthful meal chooses as you will not feel deprived, and you will be seeing results.

Now that you have the knowledge of how macronutrients and calories fuel your body, you will have a more in-depth understanding of how the foods you consume benefit you, and how intermittent fasting is working to reform your body.

Chapter 4: Intermittent Fasting Methods

One misconception with intermittent fasting is that a lot of people assume that there aren't a lot of choices that come with it. They think that they have to go whole days while starving themselves or that they are only allowed to eat one meal each day. For people who have bad eating habits or who like to eat during the day, or even for people who have issues with their blood sugar, these may seem too restricting to follow, and they may want to go with a different diet plan.

But the intermittent fasting is actually a great diet plan that has a lot of options. You can choose how many hours you ar eliminating your food intake, whether you would like to do the fasting for a bit each day or have one or two days a week where you limit your calories, and so much more.

There are a ton of options that come with the intermittent fast and part of the reason that it is so effective is that you can make the choices. You can pick the one that seems to be the most doable for your needs, pick the one that works the best for your schedule, or pick one based on some other criteria that works the best for you. This chapter is going to spend some time looking at the different options that can come available when you are on this kind of diet plan.

Don't feel like this one is going to be the most restrictive diet in the world. You are going to find that there is a lot of freedom in the times that you are fasting, how much you have to restrict yourself, and even what kinds of foods that you are allowed to eat. While you should try to eat a diet that is as healthy as possible, you will enjoy that you don't have to spend all of your time counting calories and you can even cheat a bit and have some of the sweets and more on occasion while on this diet plan.

To be successful with intermittent fasting, it is important to find a method that suits you and your lifestyle best. There numerous methods of intermittent fasting and in this chapter, we will cover some of the most popular ways we've discovered. If you start with one method and decided it is not working for you, feel free to move on and try another. Finding a weight loss method that works for you often takes time, but what matters is that you're putting in the effort. Experiment with some of these methods until you find the one you are most comfortable with. You and your body are capable of amazing things. When you are happy with your routine, you are even more capable of reaching the goals you've set for yourself!

Method 1: The 16/8 Diet – Fasting for 16 Hours a Day

The 16/8 diet is one of the most popular, sustainable and achievable methods of intermittent fasting. The 16/8 diet implements an 8-10 hour "eating window", leaving 14-16 hours for fasting. This method was developed by fitness expert Martin Berkhan and is also referred to as the Leangains method. Berkhan is a certified nutritional consultant and personal trainer. Berkhan strongly encourages supplementing this method with exercise and healthy eating.

At its foundation, the 16/8 method can be as basic as skipping breakfast, then not eating again after dinner. The best way to follow this method is by setting specific meal times during your 8-10 hour window. For example, you may set your first meal at 12pm, have a snack at 3pm, then eat dinner at 8pm. From 8pm until 12pm the next day, your body will be in its fasted state. Out of the 16 hours, you will likely be asleep for nearly half of them, meaning you'll be unbothered by, or less aware of any hunger. For those who are hungry in the morning and enjoy eating breakfast, this method may be slightly difficult to get used to, but the 16/8 diet is considered the most natural method of intermittent fasting. If you are someone who tends to skip breakfast, this method should come quite easily to you.

While this method should garner results without extreme changes to the diet, it is highly effective when exercise and healthy eating are implemented. Mark Berkhan details the 16/8 diet, or the Leangains method with exercise included. Here are a few sample setups of Berkhan's popular Leangains method:

Setup 1: Fasted Training

11:30 AM – 12 PM: 5 to 15-minute warm-up workout/pre-workout
12-1 PM: Workout routine
1 PM: First and largest meal of the day
4 PM: Second meal
9 PM: Last meal before fasting

For this setup, Berkham recommends tapering your carb intake throughout the day.

Setup 2: One Pre-Workout Meal

12-1 PM or around lunch/noon: Pre-workout meal that amounts to approximately 20-25% of daily total calorie intake.
3-4 PM: Workout routine should happen a few hours after the pre-workout meal.
4-5 PM: Second and largest meal of the day.
8-9 PM: Last meal before the fast.

Berkham often recommends this method for young adults in college, or those with flexible working hours.

Setup 3: Two Pre-Workout Meals

12-1 PM or around lunch/noon: First meal of the day that is approximately 20-25% of daily total calorie intake.

4-5 PM: Pre-workout meal that is about equal in size to the first meal.

5-6 PM: Workout routine.

8-9 PM: Last meal before the fast, and largest meal of the day.

Berkham recommends this method for those with regular working hours.

If you plan on implementing exercise in your diet, or already exercise, one of Berkham's methods will be likely to benefit you immensely. If you are not big on exercise, the 16/8 diet is still a great way to approach intermittent fasting.

Method 2: The 5:2 Diet – Low-Calorie Intake for Two Days a Week

The 5:2 diet has less of a natural flow to its pattern than the 16/8 diet, but if you are not looking to make any changes to your current diet or exercise routine, the 5:2 may get you the best results. The 5:2 diet consists of eating as your normally would during 5 days of the week, then restricting yourself to 500-600 calories during two days of the week.

The 5:2 diet was popularized by British journalist and doctor, Michael Mosley, and is often referred to as the Fast Diet. Since the 5:2 diet allows completely unmoderated eating during the 5 days out of the week, this method is great for someone looking to lose fat and gain muscle without changing the types or quantity of foods they consume drastically. Limitations on food and caloric intake will only occur two days out of the week. Your two low-calorie days should not be consecutive. Spacing out your low-calorie days is much safer and will amplify the effects of the 5:2 diet. For example, You may choose Tuesday and Friday as your low-calorie days, and eat normally on Sunday, Monday, Wednesday, Thursday and Saturday.

Being consistent with the two low-calorie days you choose is recommend to help you stay on track. Having a routine typically makes it easier for people to follow a diet plan, but it is not necessary so long as you have the right amount of discipline. It is also recommended that women on the 5:2 diet consume 500 calories on low-calorie days, and men consume 600 calories on low-calorie days for optimum results. While workout routines are not a hot topic when it comes to the 5:2 diet, exercise is always beneficial to the fat loss and muscle gain process.

Many proponents of the 5:2 diet believe it is much easier for people restrict their calories two days out of the week, rather than all seven. This method of intermittent fasting is also great for those with a hectic schedule, as meals only have to be planned out and calculated two days out of the week. Getting used such a low-calorie intake during two days of the week may be difficult to get used to, but it is very possible, and it does not have to be done perfectly right away! Tracking progress is always important when changing your eating habits, but be extra careful to track your mood, energy, and results when you begin the 5:2 diet to make sure the diet is safe and right for you. The 5:2 diet is best for those who are seeking the flexibility to eat more of the foods they enjoy while avoiding full on fasting and still getting the results they want.

Method 3: The Eat-Stop-Eat Diet – Fasting for 24 Hours Once or Twice a Week

The Eat-Stop-Eat diet is similar to the 5:2 diet, simply with much stricter fasting days. The Eat-Stop-Eat diet is another incredibly popular approach to intermittent fasting that implements one or two 24-hour long fasts during the week, with regular caloric intake during the other 5 or 6 days of the week. For example, if you planned to implement one 24-hour fast into your week, you may eat dinner at 6pm one night, then not eat again until 6pm the following day. You can also implement your fast from breakfast to the next day's breakfast, or lunch to the next day's lunch. The time of day does not really matter, so long as the fast is spanned over 24-hours. During the 24-hour fast, you are encouraged to drink water, and you may consume black coffee, some unsweetened teas, and other zero calorie beverages, but no solid foods are permitted.

The Eat-Stop-Eat diet was brought to light by fitness guru, Brad Pilon. While Pilon is a proponent of eating below a certain threshold of calories, he does not believe it is necessary to count calories on a daily basis. Pilon classifies the Eat-Stop-Eat diet as the simplest way to stay below your personal calorie threshold without precise calorie counting, depriving yourself from the foods you enjoy, or strict daily discipline. Pilon explains that the human body naturally thrives from a diet that varies between higher and lower calorie intake. In the earliest days of human existence, our ancestors ate an abundance of food when available in order to survive the times when nourishment was more difficult to find. Pilon believes that this fluctuation in food intake is still necessary, as the body is hardwired to go for short periods of time without food in between times of high caloric intake.

Along with weight loss, Brad Pilon details many other health benefits that come with the Eat-Stop-Eat method. Pilon explains that during a 24-hour fast, your body will experience an increase in fat burning hormones, a decrease in stress hormones, a boost in metabolism and energy, and a decrease in inflammation around the joints. A 24-hour fast is also said to cleanse and revitalize the body as well as increase brain functions such as memory and concentration.

When approaching intermittent fasting with the Eat-Stop-Eat method, it is recommended that you begin with 14-16 hours of fasting, then increasing the amount of time from there. A full 24-hour fast can seem very daunting. Easing yourself in is the best way to avoid getting discouraged, or feeling overwhelmed. It is normal to cave in and eat something during the later hours a 24 hour fast. It is important not to make yourself feel guilty. Negative self-talk and food guilt will only set your back further, and could quite possibly lead to more slip-ups. If you happen to go off track, accept it and move on. Do not base your self-worth or capability to meet goals on your first few 24-hour fasts. Positive reinforcement and self-talk will be much more effective on your intermittent fasting journey! The Eat-Stop-Eat diet typically takes a bit more getting used than the 16/8 diet or the 5:2 diet, as the modern individual is not acclimated to 24-hours with no food. Be sure you are comfortable with one full day of fasting per week before implementing two full days of fasting. It is also important to track your health, mood, and progress as you go. Just like other intermittent fasting methods, the Eat-Stop-Eat diet does not force changes in eating, simply the pattern of eating, but this particular method is especially complimented by healthier food chooses. Once you get the hang of it, the Eat-Stop-Eat may be implemented into your life as a long-term style of eating that works to keep you fit, young, and refreshed.

Method 4: The Alternate Day Fasting Diet – Fasting Every Other Day

The Alternate Day Fasting diet is an approach to intermittent fasting that is better suited to those who have been practicing intermittent fasting for a while. Alternate day fasting is another intermittent fasting method that draws inspiration from the eating patterns of our most ancient ancestors. As our ancient ancestors experienced times of feast and times of famine, the Alternate Day Fasting diet seeks to replicate this in order to get your body to reach its fasting state, which, as discussed, burns the fat that allows you to lose weight and gain muscle.

The Alternate Day Fasting diet can be practiced a number of different ways but there are two most common methods. One method consists of unrestricted calorie intake one day, then a full 24-hour fast the following day, continuing this pattern throughout each week. Another method of Alternate Day Fasting consists of unrestricted calorie intake one day, then an incredibly low-calorie intake the following day. For example, one may eat regularly on Monday, then limit themselves to 500-600 calories on Tuesday, then continue this pattern throughout the week.

The Alternate Day Fasting diet is an ideal way to "reboot" your metabolism, though getting used to this method takes a lot of focus and will power. The typical adjustment period when starting the Alternate Day Fasting diet is about 10 days. While the Alternate Day Fasting diet can be practiced long term, it is typically used as a short-term method to either kick start weight loss, or boost a regular intermittent fasting diet. Whether you choose to alternate between days of full fasting, or days of low-calorie intake, it is imperative to monitor your health when delving in the Alternate Day Fasting diet. Since the typical, modern person is not used to very frequent fasting, utilizing will likely throw your body off. If you are new to intermittent fasting, it may be best to ease yourself in with a method such as the 5:2 diet or the Eat-Stop-Eat diet. It is important to practice the Alternate Day Fasting diet safely, and healthily. You may even gear your alternate fasting days to better suit your needs. For example, you may eat regularly Sunday, do a full 24-hour fast on Monday, eat regularly on Tuesday, then on Wednesday restrict your calorie intake to 500-600 calories.

The Alternate Day Fasting diet is easily modified, but with no modification or light modification, it is likely to produce results more quickly than other methods. If you are seeking fast results that can be achieved without changes to the types and quantities of foods you consume, the Alternate Day Fasting diet is a great choice for you. If you plan on practicing Alternate Day Fasting short term for kick started weight loss, be careful to find the best method to maintain your results once you complete your preferred length of time with the diet. If you plan to practice the Alternate Day Fasting diet long term, be sure this method is safe and healthy for you and your body. Adjusting to an Alternate Day Fasting diet may take time, but perseverance and positivity will keep you motivated and on track.

Method 5: The Warrior Diet – Eating One Huge Meal at Night

The Warrior diet is a great approach to intermittent fasting for those who are not looking to participate in full 24-hour fasts. The Warrior diet consists of eating small amounts of raw fruits and vegetable throughout the day, then consuming one very large meal at night. The foundation of the Warrior diet is to fast all day, then feast within a 4-hour window in the evening.

The Warrior diet was popularized by Ori Hofmekler, a well-known nutrition expert and fitness guru. Unlike a number of other intermittent fasting methods, Ori Hofmekler's version of the Warrior diet places emphasis on food choice and exercise. In terms of the encouraged food choices, the Warrior diet is comparable to a paleo diet which consists of whole, unprocessed foods that appear as they would in nature when consumed. Since Hofmekler's Warrior diet incorporates intermittent fasting, the food regulations are much less strict than that of a paleo diet, but whole, organic eating is encouraged.

In Ori Hofmekler's book, *The Warrior Diet*, he explains that a regular exercise routine truly compliments the eating method. Hofmekler encourages a full body, 20-minute to 45-minute workout be conducted during fasting times. In his book, Hofmekler also suggests alternating between fat-centric and carbohydrate centric meals, as well as eating carbohydrates last during daily meals to in order balance insulin levels, and cutting down on consumption of alcohol.

In *The Warrior Diet*, Hofmekler explains the controlled fatigue system, which most basically consists of a person conducting a workout when they are already fatigued. Hofmekler details the process of the controlled fatigue initiating the body's "fight or flight" response which inherently promotes weight loss and muscle gain.

While Ori Hofmekler's Warrior diet has much more strict guidelines than the methods we've discussed, it can be modified and practiced in a way that you feel suits you best. For example, you may fast the entire day then eat an unrestricted meal with your choice of food at night. Even if you do not change your food choices immediately, it is likely you will see results from the Warrior diet due to the change in your eating pattern. The Warrior diet the perfect approach to intermittent fasting for those who are interested in making changes to their current diet and workout routine. Paired with frequent exercise and healthful food choices, the Warrior diet should show results very quickly. While results should still be apparent without exercise or modifying your diet, changes may occur more slowly with the Warrior diet.

Method 6: Spontaneous Meal Skipping - Skipping Meals When Possible or Convenient

The Spontaneous Meal Skipping method is one of the least involved methods of intermittent fasting as it does not require a set structure or drastic pattern change. Most of have even participated in Spontaneous Meal Skipping without even realizing it. Spontaneous Meal Skipping simply consists of skipping meals when you do not feel hungry or if you are too busy to eat. For example, if you do not feel hungry one morning, skip breakfast and eat lunch when you feel you are ready. If you are having a very busy day and lunch slips your mind, avoid eating until dinner time. If you are in search of a snack, but can't find anything appetizing, participate in a short fast instead.

Spontaneous Meal Skipping often occurs unconsciously, but it is a surprisingly effective method of intermittent fasting when practiced with basic healthy eating. While Spontaneous Meal Skipping does not quite allow for unrestricted calorie intake during meal times, it does take your body into a fasted state you would not normally reach without skipping meals. Spontaneous Meal Skipping makes it easier to say yes to your cravings while still seeing weight loss and muscle gain.

With a bit of conscious effort, the Spontaneous Meal Skipping method may be a great place, to begin with intermittent fasting. It is also a great way to supplement your current diet without making any drastic changes. Spontaneous Meal Skipping is a very convenient form of intermittent fasting that will likely show results if practiced frequently.

Method 7: The Fat Loss Forever Diet – One "Cheat Day" Followed by a 36-Hour Fast

The Fat Loss Forever diet is a highly structured form of intermittent fasting. The Fat Loss Forever diet combines bits of the Leangains or 16/8 method, the Eat-Stop-Eat diet, and the Warrior diet, creating a method of intermittent fasting that is geared toward exercise lovers who don't want to give up their favorite foods.

The Fat Loss Forever diet was popularized by fitness experts John Romaniello and Dan Go. While Romaniello and Go developed a meticulous, seven-day food and exercise guide for their method, the foundation of the Fat Loss Forever diet consists of structured, healthy eating over the first 5 days out of the week, indulging or "cheating" over half of the 6th day, then fasting for a full 36-hours following your "cheat day". For example, you may restrict your calories and participate in short-term fasts from Monday – Friday, then indulge from 8AM to 8PM on Saturday, then fasting from 8PM until breakfast on Monday. Romaniello and Go suggest doing the full 36-hour fast during your busiest day of the week in order to distract you from hunger. Non-caloric beverages such as water, black coffee, and zero calorie teas are encouraged during the 36-hour fast. This method is highly involved and is almost solely recommended for those who are experienced with intermittent fasting patterns. In Romaniello and Go's Fat Loss Forever plan, exercise is greatly emphasized, so this method is suited for those who already exercise in their typical routine or are looking to incorporate exercise into their lifestyle.

The Fat Loss Forever diet is a great method of intermittent fasting for those who thrive when sticking to a set schedule and clear guidelines. While the Fat Loss Forever diet is not for everyone, practicing the method short term may be the most effective way to lose those last few stubborn pounds you can't seem to shake.

As you can see, there are many ways to approach intermittent fasting, so finding one that suits you, your goals and your lifestyle is completely possible. If you are new to intermittent fasting, the 16/8 diet may be the easiest to get the hang of. If you're big on exercise, the Warrior diet may be the one for you, if you're always on the go, Spontaneous Meal Skipping may be the best way for you to break into intermittent fasting. No matter your size, shape, or lifestyle, there is a method of intermittent fasting that will suit you and help you achieve the results you want!

Chapter 5: The Health Benefits of Going on an Intermittent Fast

One of the best benefits that comes from going on the intermittent fast is that you are going to feel so much better with your health. Many Americans suffer from a lot of health issues, from diabetes, too much weight, heart issues, and so much more. You will find that the diet that most Americans enjoy, from eating out all the time, eating foods that are too bad and eating too much of these foods, is causing them to gain weight and feel miserable all the time.

The issues with the American diet are part of the reason that there are so many fad diets out there. These diets are promising that they will help the person lose a lot of weight quickly and help them to get their health back better than before. But many of them are trying to offer help just so that they can make money and the person is going to feel like a failure when they aren't able to succeed on these unhealthy diets.

The intermittent fasting diet is better because it is not a fad, it is a way of life, changing some of the habits that you have rather than limiting the foods that you are allowed to eat. While you do need to limit some of the unhealthy options that you are consuming in your diet and focus more on the nutrition that you need, you will not have to focus so much on the types of foods that you are eating or the amount of calories that you are going with. This can take away some of the stress of being on a diet and is one of the things that you are going to love when you are working on losing weight and getting healthier.

Because you are going to be eating fewer calories and tricking your body to burn more calories without having to do more work, you will find that it is easier to get the good health that you want. The intermittent fasting is going to help you to lose weight without all the extra work, get your heart in the best shape ever, lower your risk of diabetes, and so much more. Add in a good workout program (which we will discuss some more in a later chapter), and you are sure to see the good health results that you want.

- Lose weight—one of the main reasons that a lot of people choose to do an intermittent fast is to lose weight. They are not happy with their current weight and all of the bad health effects that are around because of it and they are ready to make a change that is safe and makes sense for their bodies. You will find that the intermittent fast can be really effective at helping you to lose weight. It will limit how much you are allowed to eat each day while still making you feel satisfied and like you are getting plenty to eat all the time. In addition, it is tricking the body to burn through more calories than ever before so while you are eating less, you are also going to be burning more calories, making weight loss easier than ever before.

- Lower your blood sugars—when you are following the traditional American diet, it is highly likely that you are on the verge of dealing with issues with diabetes. Most Americans are taking in more of the sugars and processed carbs that are causing damage to all parts of their bodies and making them the next candidate for diabetes. The intermittent fast is going to help you to control some of your cravings so that you are able to get back on track. You will learn how to regulate the blood sugars, how to eat fewer of the bad carbs and the sugars that are causing the issues in the first place and to eat a healthier diet that will keep diabetes at bay for you.

- Lower heart issues—your heart should be precious to you. It is the part of the body that is going to help you to feel good, to keep on moving, and provides blood to all the other parts of the body. If the heart is not in good working condition, you will notice that everything is going to suffer as a result. When you eat the traditional American diet (the one that is full of too many calories, too many fats, and too many sugars and sodium), you are doing a number on your heart. You are dealing with higher cholesterol levels and even higher blood pressure due to the foods that you eat. With the help of the intermittent fast, you will be able to limit some of the harm of those bad foods by eliminating them, and it is easier than before to get the heart back to the good health that you want.

- Lower stroke risks—when you take care of your heart, you are going to reduce the risk of stroke over the long term. When you are eating a bad diet with lots of fats, sugars, and other bad things, along with all those extra calories that are hard on the body, you are forcing the heart to work harder than it should. Add on the issues with high blood cholesterol, and you are sure to end up with a lot of stress on the heart, which can lead to a higher risk of stroke. When it comes to working on the intermittent fasting diet, though, you will find that eating healthier foods, and restricting how often you are able to eat throughout the day, can help you to develop some healthier habits that are good for the heart and can lower your risk of developing a stroke.

- Mental clarity—are you one of those people who have trouble remembering things or feel like your head is always in some kind of a fog at the end of the day? It may be time to make some changes to the foods that you are eating. Like the rest of your body, your brain needs to be fed the right kinds of foods in order to stay healthy and happy for the long term. While this may seem like a hard thing to accomplish, using the intermittent fast, along with the healthier foods that you should be eating on this diet plan, can help you to feed the brain the right nutrition that it needs and ensures that you are able to think clearly much more than before.

- More energy—when you start eating foods that are healthier and better for you, it is easier to think more clearly. You will find that a lot of the bad foods you have been eating are holding you down. Rather than letting these bad foods cloud your memory and make it harder to get things done during the day. With the healthy foods that you will be able to eat when you are on the intermittent fast, you will be able to not only increase the mental clarity, but you can provide a lot of the good nutrition that the body needs in order to feel great and like you are ready to take on the world. When you are tired of having trouble getting out of bed each day, and you can barely make it past lunchtime without needing a nap, it may be time to try out the intermittent fasting diet and see how well it is going to work on your energy.

As you can see, there are quite a few benefits that you will be able to enjoy when it comes to going on this diet plan. While a lot of the other diets that you can try out will promise to give you the same benefits, none of them are going to work quite like the intermittent fasting diet, and none of them are going to be near as easy to follow. If you are just able to change up some of the eating habits that you have and make them work with this fast, you will find that losing weight and enjoying all the health benefits does not have to be such a pain any longer.

Chapter 6: Dieting And Weight Loss Myths Dispelled

Throughout the history of dieting and nutrition, dieting and weight loss myths have run rampant through books, televisions programs, and word of mouth. Many weight loss and dieting myths have no proof to back them up, and some myths could even be hurting you rather than helping you on your weight loss journey. In this chapter, we will expel some of the most prominent dieting and weight loss myths, so you know just what to believe, and just what to discredit.

Myth 1: Don't Eat After 8PM

One of the most common things you'll hear when you diet is that eating at night, or after 8PM will cause you to gain weight, or prevent you from losing weight. The idea behind this myth is that food you eat early in the day is burned up during your daily activities, but food you consume at night sits dormant in your system while you sleep, and therefore turns into fat. This myth became very prominent because the concept behind it seems logical.

Many night time eaters tend to overeat, or make unhealthy choices due to tiredness. While this can lead to weight gain or prevent weight loss, it is not due to the time that food is consumed. The fact is, eating at night or after 8PM will not affect your weight. The truth is, calories can't tell time, and your body processes the food you eat in the same way regardless of what time of day it is.

An effective intermittent fasting method like the Warrior diet truly expels this myth. When practiced properly, the Warrior diet results in muscle gain and weight loss even though the biggest meal of the day is consumed at night.

Myth 2: Eating Small Meals Frequently Throughout the Day Will Boost your Metabolism

One popular dieting and weight loss misconception is that eating small, but frequent meals throughout your day will give your metabolism a boost and help you burn calories faster. The explanation behind this concept is that that the more frequently you consume food, the more often your metabolism will have to work to burn it. This concept is comparable to a wood burning fire, as it basically states the more fuel you add to your body, the harder your body will have to work to burn it. This truth is, food consumption has very little effect on your metabolic rate.

While some foods may slightly boost your metabolism, like foods and beverages that contain caffeine, the effect is not quite significant enough to speed up your metabolism permanently or promote weight loss. Your basal metabolic rate, or BMR, is based on the rate in which your body burns calories when in a resting state. Typically, the more muscle mass you have, the more calories you burn overall. One pound of muscle typically burns 14 calories per day. Intermittent fasting expels this myth overall, as each proven approach practices eating larger meals less often throughout the day.

An effective intermittent fasting method that incorporates exercise such as the Leangains diet or the Fat Loss Forever diet is a great way to burn fat, gain muscle and naturally boost the metabolism as you go.

Myth 3: Carbohydrates Make You Fat

As discussed in Chapter 2, many recent fad diets and dieting trends have suggested cutting carbohydrates completely out of your eating routine. These trendy diets perpetuated the myth that carbohydrates were the case of weight gain. This is not true. This myth, like many, stemmed from the statistic. Proteins and fats cause weight gain just as easily as carbohydrates, and while many people overeat when it comes to all three macronutrients, most people tend to overeat carbohydrates. While the body does take carbohydrates and turn them into sugars, they are not immediately stored as fat as this myth often suggests.

Carbohydrates are a necessary source of nutrition for the human body, and many of our healthiest foods are categorized as carbohydrates. Whole grains, fruits, and vegetables are classified as carbohydrates. Avoiding carbohydrates entirely is not only unhealthy, but it is also not an effective weight loss method. Rather than cutting carbohydrates out, enjoy carbohydrates in moderation, choose healthier carbohydrates, or indulge in carbohydrates on your unrestricted intermittent fasting days.

The trick here is to make sure that you are eating the right kinds of carbs. If you are getting all your carbs from highly processed foods, such as pizza, pasta, donuts, baked goods and more, you are going to see that your weight is gong to gain in no time. These are often going to be full of calories and lots of sugars that will not go away and can add on the weight. These not only have a lot of the bad stuff, but also no nutritional benefits, so you are just feeding your body a lot of junk.

On the other hand, if you make sure that you are eating the right carbs along the way, such as whole wheat and whole grain, you will find that you are getting a lot of the nutrition that your body needs. These are full of a lot of great b-vitamins and more to make sure that you are staying healthy as possible. Make sure to eat the good carbs, the ones that can fuel your body, and you will find that they are actually going to help you to lose weight.

Myth 4: Coffee Makes You Skinny

One frequently perpetuated weight loss myth is that drinking coffee can make you lose weight. The idea behind this concept is that coffee acts as an appetite suppressant, as well as a metabolism booster due to its high caffeine content. While caffeine does speed up the metabolism, the effect is minimal, and its appetite suppressing effects tend to wear off quickly. While a cup or two of coffee may help to make you feel full, the caffeine content isn't really enough to influence noticeable weight loss. Drinking excessive amounts of coffee may put you at risk for anxiety, sleeplessness, high blood pressure, or increased heart rate.

One to three cups of coffee per day depending on your caffeine tolerance can be helpful in squelching your appetite for a few hours, but relying on coffee for weight loss is not a very viable or safe method.

This may be a bit hard for a few people to handle, especially if you are a big coffee lover and want to believe that you will be able to lose weight while enjoying your favorite drink. But it is not really any more effective at quenching your thirst than water or any other option, and the calories inside will sometimes ruin some of the other nutrition that you can get. If you are already drinking coffee, keep it down to a few cups a day or less. But if you have never drank coffee and don't enjoy it, you shouldn't feel like you need to get started because it doesn't make that much of a difference in your weight loss.

Myth 5: Breakfast is the Most Important Meal of the Day

For years, nutritionist and fitness gurus have sworn by the idea that breakfast is the most important meal of the day. The idea that eating breakfast is directly linked to weight loss stems from a number of different ideas. Many of them stem from cultural and behavioral norms. Breakfast has culturally accepted as a necessary meal for decades upon decades. While many people do feel they benefit from eating breakfast, many others force themselves to eat breakfast because they believe they have to. Another idea behind this concept is that, if you eat a big breakfast it will be burnt off throughout the day. The myth that breakfast is the most important meal of the day can easily be attributed to the rampant idea that there is only one "right" way to eat or only one "correct path" to weight loss. While breakfast may be an important meal for some, recent studies show that, in terms of weight loss and health, eating breakfast is not at all necessary.

Two studies published by the US National Library of Medicine, scientists found no direct link between weight loss and consuming breakfast. Your body is programmed to burn calories at the same rate throughout the day, regardless of what time it is. Much like how eating at night does not necessarily affect weight loss or gain, whether you begin eating in the morning or afternoon does not really make a difference in your fat burning mechanisms or your metabolic rate. While studies dispelled the myth that eating breakfast is linked to weight loss, the same studies did find a link between weight loss and pushing breakfast back into the afternoon hours. If you feel eating breakfast boosts your energy or focus, continue to do so, but if you feel breakfast makes you sluggish, or if you find that eating breakfast does not fit in with you intermittent fasting method, feel free to skip it and begin eating in the afternoon.

Myth 6: Milk Helps You Lose Weight

Though not as rampant as many other dieting and weight loss myths, the rumor that milk can help you lose weight has been spread throughout numerous books, articles, and television programs. The idea behind this concept is that the calcium in milk helps the body to break down fat more effectively, therefore promoting and speeding up weight loss. Numerous studies concluded that milk and dairy did not have any prominent weight loss effects.

While drinking milk and consuming dairy may not speed up the fat loss process, they will still contribute you to your necessary calcium intake. If you are lactose intolerant or practice a vegan diet, calcium can be obtained through fortified soy milk, fortified orange juice, leafy greens such as kale, and even through certain types of fish.

Drinking milk is not necessarily a bad thing all the time. It does help you tog et the calcium, vitamin D, and more that you will need in order to stay healthy and happy, but you won't necessarily be able to lose any extra weight when you are drinking it. If you do add it into your diet (and there are a ton of great food products that you are able to consume that can give you the calcium that you need without having milk), make sure that you are sticking with the lower calorie options so that you skip out on some of the saturated fats and other options that are in the higher fat versions.

Myth 7: Cutting Calories Drastically is Necessary for Weight Loss

Cutting calories have always been one of the most widely accepted methods of pursuing weight loss. While cutting and counting calories is an effective method for weight loss, it is not sustainable for the average person. Drastically cutting calories often makes a person feel deprived. This frequently leads to short-term results that are quickly obliterated due to shifting back to regular eating habits. Many studies show that extremely low-calorie diet can lead to digestive issues, gallstones, and long-term health issues.

While calories do matter, intermittent fasting expels the myth that a radical decrease in the number of calories you consume is necessary to drop weight. Maintaining your current calorie intake but changing your eating pattern to fit the intermittent fasting method of your choice can be more effective than extreme calorie cutting, and can easily produce more long term results.

The more important thing here is not always how many calories you are cutting out; it is more about the types of foods that you are eating. If you are eating foods that are healthy and have a lot of nutrients, you will be able to eat more calories compared to just eating a lot of junk.

It is also important to remember that you do need to have a specific amount of calories coming in each day. Your body is not able to function if it doesn't receive enough calories to get things done and doing this over the long term can be dangerous to your health. While missing out on some calories for a few days here or there, such as when you are sick, is not the end of the world, you shouldn't do this on a regular basis. It is much better to focus on eating healthy foods, rather than drastically limiting your calories, to ensure that you are going to lose weight and stay as healthy as possible.

There are a lot of diet myths that are out there. Some of these are just brought about by a misunderstanding of how things work with the body and dieting, and others are there because of the misinformation that is being spread around by diet companies and products that are trying to sell things. Learn what is actually healthy for your body and stick with that and you are going to see the best results possible.

Chapter 7: Sample Meal Plans And Food Suggestions

Intermittent fasting makes it incredibly easy to modify your food choices in order to make the diet of your choice work for you. While intermittent fasting does offer quite a bit of freedom, a food plan or standard guide may help you stay on track or, at the very least, give you a loose outline to follow. In this chapter, we will give sample food plans for the most popular intermittent fasting methods.

Food Plan 1: Works Best with the Leangains or 16/8 Method

First Meal (After Workout)
4 palm sizes of grilled chicken breast
3 fist full sizes of your choice of vegetable
About 100 grams of whole grains
1/2 handful of raw almonds
1/2 handful of green peas
2 cups of drinking water

Second Meal (About 3-4 Hours Later)
3 palms size of salmon
3 fist full sizes of your choice of vegetable
About 50 grams of whole grains
1/2 handful of raw cashews

1/2 handful of black beans
2 cups of drinking water

Third Meal (About 4-5 Hours Later)
2 palm sizes of ground turkey
2 fist full of your choice of vegetables
About 50 grams of whole grains
1/2 handful of macadamia nuts
2 cups of drinking water

Suggested Daily Supplements
1 multi-vitamin
4000 IU vitamin D
1 tablespoon fish oil
10 g BCAA capsules before workouts

This basic meal plan is a great foundation for practicing the Leangains or 16/8 method. This outline shows about how much of each macronutrient you should be consuming on a daily basis, but can easily be modified to include the foods you love, and allow you satisfy your cravings during your eating window.

Food Plan 2: Works Best with The Warrior Diet Method

Wake Up Meal
Large Glass of Water
Three Brazil Nuts
1 cup of black coffee

1 handful of raw almonds
1 vitamin D supplement
Total calories – 250

First Snack of the Day (1-2 Hours Later)
1 cup of black coffee
1 handful of blackberries
Casein protein shake mixed in water
Total calories– 170

Second Snack of the Day (2-3 Hours Later)
Casein protein shake mixed in water
1 handful of Blackberries
Total Calories – 170

Work Suggested to Take Place Immediately After this Snack (Around 5PM)

Post Workout Protein Shake (Around 6:30PM)
1 cup almond milk
1 cup organic tart cherry juice
1 handful of ice cubes
1 scoop of whey protein
1 half scoop casein
1 very large scoop of peanut butter
TOTAL – 610 Calories

Main Feast Meal (Around 7PM)
1 serving of fresh vegetables

1 serving of cooked vegetables
1 large helping of animal protein such as steak, chicken, or pork
1 serving of potatoes, prepared to your liking
1 multivitamin

Second Main Feast Meal (Around 9:30PM)
Six scrambled eggs
Total calories – 420

This basic meal plan is a great foundation for practicing the Warrior diet method. While this outline focuses on days that include workouts, rest day meal plans may suggest a lower calorie feast for your final meal of the day. The main feast is meant to differ from day to day to your liking to keep you from feeling deprived or cut off from the foods you enjoy. Make sure to change up your food choices every now and then when practicing this method.

Many of the intermittent fasting methods discussed in this book consist of unrestricted eating days paired with days of full fasting or low-calorie intake days. On full fasting days, water, black coffee, and zero calorie teas are encouraged. However, low-calorie intake days may be a bit a trickier in terms of figuring out what to eat. The following meals fit within a 500-600 total calorie count range and work very well with the 5:2 diet, the Eat-Stop-Eat diet, the Alternate Day Fasting diet, and others.

Meal Suggestions for 500-600 Calorie Fasting Days

First Meal:
40 grams of oat porridge

Second Meal:
Beet root and feta salad
50 grams of beetroot
30 grams of feta cheese
60 grams of spinach
1 squeeze of lemon

Third Meal:
Sliced apple
1 tablespoon of almond butter
Total calorie count: 525

First Meal:
2 sweet plums
100 grams of low-fat natural yogurt
1 teaspoon of honey

Second Meal:
Ryvita and tuna slices
2 Ryvita crackerbreads
60 grams of tuna mayo
Cracked black pepper

Third Meal:

Miso soup
Total calorie count: 430

First Meal:
1 egg
5 pieces of asparagus
Salt and cracked black pepper

Second Meal:
Bunless turkey burgers
111 grams of turkey mince (beat with one small egg, spring onion, garlic, and chili)
1 corn on the cob

Third Meal:
A few frozen grapes
Total calorie count: 478 calories

First Meal:
Spinach omelet
2 scrambled eggs
60 grams of spinach greens
Salt and cracked black pepper

Second Meal:
40 grams of hummus
Carrots
Cucumbers
Cracked black pepper

Third Meal:
60 grams of edamame beans
Rock salt
Total calorie count: 419

First Meal:
100 grams of low-fat natural yogurt
1 sliced banana
Small sprinkle of cinnamon

Second Meal:
125 grams of turkey breast steak
1 cup of spinach, cooked and seasoned with salt

Third Meal:
10 grams of popcorn
Total calorie count: 452

First Meal:
1 red or green apple
1 carrot - 52
Raw ginger

Second Meal:
Pita pizza
Whole grain pita
25 grams of extra light cream cheese
1 Roma tomato - 32 calories

Mixed herbs
Salt and cracked black pepper

Third Meal:
100 grams of blueberries
One large handful of almonds
Total calorie count: 422

First Meal:
Mixed berry bowl
100 grams of raw strawberries
100 grams of raw raspberries
100 grams of raw blueberries

Second Meal:
Harissa chicken with chargrilled vegetable couscous
130 grams of grilled chicken breast
100 grams of vegetable couscous
1 tablespoon harissa paste

Third Meal:
About 10 unshelled pistachio nuts - 60 calories
Total calorie count - 489 calories

First Meal:
3 Weightwatchers low calories blueberry buttermilk pancakes

Second Meal:

Roasted red pepper and tomato soup with Ryvita crackerbreads
2 original Ryvita crackerbreads
1 half of a red pepper, 1 half of a Roma tomato, 1 half of an onion, 1 diced garlic clove, 1 teaspoon of tomato puree, 1 half teaspoon of cumin, one chicken stock cube, 1 half teaspoon of balsamic vinegar, 1 half teaspoon of salt and cracked black pepper to season

Third Meal:
1 half tablespoon of pumpkin seeds
1 half tablespoon of sunflower seeds
Total calorie count: 424 calories

First meal:
50 grams of fruit and nut muesli

Second Meal:
Pesto salmon with curly kale
100 grams of salmon fillet
3 teaspoons of green pesto
100 grams of steamed kale, seasoned with cracked black pepper

Third Meal:
60 grams of stoned cherries
Total calorie count: 506 calories

Remember, it is not necessary to adhere perfectly to the meal plans detailed here. These are simply samples and suggestions meant to outline the nutrients your body requires for proper functioning, as well as ideas for what to eat and when to eat it. Intermittent fasting is a method that is meant to be modified to suit and satisfy your dietary needs. Avoid depriving yourself or forcing yourself to stick to an unrealistic meal plan. Restricting yourself on days that are meant for unrestricted calorie intake or indulging could likely lead to feeling discouraging or falling off track. The point of intermittent fasting is to allow you to say yes to your cravings while losing weight and gaining muscle in an easy to understand and enjoyable way.

Chapter 8: Beginners Workout Plan

In addition to making sure that you are eating the right foods and eating them at the right times to help you to lose weight, you will also need to make sure that you are working on the right workout program to ensure that you are able to burn some more calories, keep the metabolism going strong, and to make sure that you are building those strong muscles that you really want.

If you have never done a good workout plan for muscle building in the past, you should start out with this chapter to ensure that you are getting started and that you aren't overdoing it. Once you get some experience with some of these new moves and you start to see some of the bulk that you are looking for with the moves as well as the new way of eating, you will find that the more advanced workout will be a good place to head next. Let's take a look at a simple workout plan that you are able to follow to start seeing some more of the results that you want with this diet plan.

The Workout Plan

With this set of workout plans, we are going to start out slowly and work on some of the bigger muscle movements that you need in order to get all the strength and muscle tone that you are looking for. We are going to work on some higher weight with fewer repetitions (meaning that you won't do a hundred of each move at a time) in order to really stretch out those muscle fibers and to ensure that you are going to get the lean and toned muscle that you are looking for.

Monday

(all of these should be done for 15 reps. You will do three sets with a rest that is about a minute long between each of the sets).
- Bodyweight squats—this one should have no weights as a beginner, just start with doing a correct squat without weights.
- Dumbbell bench press

- Pull-up

- Dumbbell deadlift

- Dumbbell lateral raise

- Hammer curl

- Triceps push down

- Bicycle crunch

- Cardio for five to fifteen minutes—you can choose the type of cardio that you are doing, but some good examples are rowing, cycling, elliptical trainer, walk, or jog.

Tuesday

(for these, you are going to do 12 reps with three sets on each of the exercises. Make sure to take a rest of a minute between each of the sets).

- Dumbbell incline bench press

- Bodyweight or dumbbell step-up

- Dumbbell bent over row

- Bodyweight or dumbbell lunge

- Dumbbell seating shoulder press

- Plank—this one you will hold the plank for 60 seconds each, doing three reps.

- Spend five to fifteen minutes doing some kind of cardio again.

Wednesday

Take a day off here to rest. If you feel like working out, spend 30 minutes or so doing a light cardio, such as going for a walk or a jog to stretch out the muscles and give them a bit of a break.

Thursday

(these workouts are going to need three sets with 15 reps each. Make sure to take a minute break in between each set.)

- Dumbbell split squat

- Power clean

- Parallel bar dip

- Incline reverse fly

- Lying leg raise

- Seated calf raise

- EZ bar curl

- Close grip bench press

- Spend five to fifteen minutes doing some kind of cardio

Friday

(for these workouts, you will do 3 sets with 12 reps in each. Take a break of a minute in between each set).

- Dumbbell squat

- Chin-up

- Dumbbell chest fly

- Dumbbell upright row

- Single arm dumbbell row

- Good morning

- Spend five to fifteen minutes doing some cardio

You should stick with this program for about two months. This allows you to start seeing some of the gains that you want plus you are going to get some of the benefits from increasing the weights and taking on more to make sure that the muscles start to grow more than before.

How to Progress This Program

Phase 1:

During the first phase, you should follow the outline above for about two months. If you feel that you have some experience with weight lifting to start with and you notice after a few weeks that your fitness progression and growth are becoming stagnant, it may be time to make things a bit more difficult on the body and you will need to move over to Phase 2. While working in Phase 1, you should try to increase the weight by about 2 to 7 percent each week or add in some weights to the body weight portions to make them a bit tougher.

Phase 2:

This one should last for about a month or so depending on your progress and what your overall goals are about. For this one, you will want to switch over to just doing 12 reps instead of the 15. While this may seem easier, you will want to increase the amount of weight that you are using. You will want to increase the weights by about 10 to 15 percent depending on what you are comfortable with and only take a short rest, not going above 60 seconds in between each one.

Phase 3:

This one should last about six weeks depending on how comfortable you feel with the weights and how much you are progressing overall. This one you will want to do about 10 reps in each set rather than the 12 you were doing before. You will also want to increase the amount of sets that you are doing from three to four and then just rest for about 45 seconds in between each of the sets. Take a look at the amount of weight that you were dealing with in the second phase and then add another 10 to 15 percent if possible.

This is a great beginners exercise plan that you can work with. If you have never done weight lifting or are not that familiar with working out at all in the first place, you will find that this one is going to give you some of the results that you want. Keep in mind that you should go at your own pace. If you need to spend three months or more in the first phase before you are comfortable moving on, that is fine. Just work at your own pace to get the results that you want.

Chapter 9: Advanced Workout Plan

After you have had some time to do the more beginner workout that was in the previous chapter, it is time to move on to one that is more advanced. Also, if you have had some time to work on weight lifting in the past or are a good workout person, you may find that starting with the more advanced plan is going to make things easier for you. If you are ready to do some more advanced workouts, take a look at this workout plan to finally see some of the results that you want along with the Intermittent Fasting diet.

Note: you should do each of these on a different day of the week, usually focusing on one upper body and one of the lower body ones before taking a break and finishing out the week with the other two. Also, alternate between the upper body and the lower body so that you are giving the muscles a break before hitting it hard again.

Upper Body A

1. Bench press

    a. 3 sets with 6 to 8 reps in each one

    b. Rest for 2 minutes between the sets.

2. Rows

   a. 3 sets with 6 to 8 reps in each one

   b. Rest for 2 minutes between sets

3. Incline dumbbell press

   a. 3 sets with 8 to 10 reps

   b. Rest for 1 minute between each set.

4. Lat pull downs

   a. 3 sets with 8 to 10 reps each

   b. Rest for a minute between each set

5. Lateral raises

   a. 2 sets with 10 to 12 reps in each one

   b. Take one minute of rest in between each set.

6. Triceps press downs

   a. 2 sets with 10 to 12 reps in each one

   b. Take one minute of rest in between each rest.

7. Dumbbell curls

   a. 2 sets with 10 to 12 reps in each one

   b. Take a minute rest between each set.

Lower Body A

1. Romanian deadlifts

    a. 3 sets with 6 to 8 reps each

    b. Rest for 2 minutes between each set

2. Leg press

    a. 3 sets with 10 to 12 reps in each

    b. Rest for 1 minute between each set

3. Seated leg curls

    a. 3 sets with 8 to 10 reps in each

    b. Rest for a minute between sets

4. Standing calf raises

    a. 4 sets with 6 to 8 reps in each

    b. Rest for 1 minute between the sets

5. Abs

    a. Do ten minutes of abs at the end of this workout.

Upper Body B

1. Pull ups

   a. 3 sets with 6 to 8 reps each

   b. Rest for 2 minutes between the sets

2. Barbell shoulder press

   a. 3 sets with 6 to 8 reps in each

   b. Take a 2-minute rest between the sets.

3. Seated cable row

   a. 3 sets with 8 to 10 reps

   b. Rest for 1 minute between each of the sets.

4. Dumbbell bench press

   a. 3 sets with 8 to 10 reps each

   b. Rest for 1 minute between each set

5. Dumbbell fly

   a. 2 sets with 10 to 12 reps each

   b. 1 minute of rest between each of the sets

6. Barbell curls

   a. 2 sets with 10 to 12 reps

   b. Rest for 1 minute between the sets

7. Skull crushers

a. 2 sets with 10 to 12 reps each

b. Rest for 1 minute between each set.

Lower Body B

1. Squats

    a. 3 sets with 6 to 8 reps each

    b. Rest for 2 minutes between each set

2. Split squats

    a. 3 sets with 8 to 10 reps each

    b. Rest for 1 minute between the sets

3. Laying leg curls

    a. 3 sets with 10 to 12 reps each

    b. Rest for 1 minute between each set.

4. Seated calf raises

    a. 4 sets with 10 to 12 reps

    b. Rest for 1 minute between each set

5. Abs

    a. Do abs for about 10 minutes at the end of the program.

After you are done with all of the sets that you are going to do each day with the upper and lower bodies, take some time to do a bit of cardio. It doesn't have to be too intense and going for fifteen minutes or less and just enough to help you to get the heart rate up a little bit higher than before. This can help to trim the fat even more while working on the muscles and is good for your heart, helps to lower health risks, and so much more.

This workout plan can last you for as long as you would like, but often works well for a few months. You can always add on more weights and a different amount of repetitions and sets to make it more challenging and to make the workout more effective in terms of the results that you are going to get.

Chapter 10: Tips for Getting the Most Out of Working Out with Intermittent Fasting

When you are first getting started with weight lifting, you are probably pretty excited. You want to make sure that you are able to get all the benefits of a nice lean body with some great muscles in place, but you are worried that you are not going to be able to do it right. Some people get too excited about what they are doing, and they assume that they should do the heaviest weight, and work out for hours each da, in order to see the results that they want. Others may feel that it is too hard and the are going to get too much bulk out of the work that they are doing.

In this chapter, we are going to spend some time looking at the tips that you need to get the most out of your workout goals. Whether you are a beginner, or you are looking to get more out of your workouts so that the intermittent fast can be more successful than before, make sure to check out some of these great tips and get started with your new weight lifting goals without having to worry about hurting yourself or missing out on the results that you want.

- Start out slow—if you have never done a weight lifting program before, you will need to start out slowly. Even if you have done some cardio workouts in the past, these are going to be a bit different compared to what you are used to. Give your muscles a bit of time to adjust, and you will start to add on more weights and get into the more challenging stuff before you know it.

- Add more weight when you feel comfortable—it is important to consistently add on more weights when you start to feel comfortable. Over time, the weights that you begin your workout with is going to start to feel pretty light, and if you don't make some changes, you will find that your results are going to slow down. The workouts above are going to give you some suggestions on what you are able to do when it comes to adding on more weight, but make sure to add on the weights at regular intervals to keep the gains coming.

- Fewer reps and more weight is best for lean muscles— when you are looking to get some of the leaner muscle in your body, it is best to work with a higher weight but fewer reps. This can exhaust the body faster and will give you the results that you are looking for.

- Do a warm up and cool down—no matter how much weight you are going to do in your workout, you should take some time to do a warm-up and a cool down. These don't have to last for too long. Usually about five minutes or so for both of them can make a big difference. These help to get the body ready to do a workout and ensures that it has some time to rest before stopping.

- Find a good tempo to stay safe—each person is going to have a tempo that they follow when they are at the gym. Some like to go slower and enjoy their time, giving the muscles some time to relax in between before hitting it hard again. Others like to go through it a bit faster. You should find the tempo that seems the most comfortable for you and keep in mind that safety should always come first.

- Focus on the form—sometimes we get too focused on how much weight we are holding when we do this kind of workout. But the form that you are doing is actually more important. It is better to do it with the right form with lower weight than to add on more weight and do it in the wrong form. Doing the wrong form with too much weight may seem like it is going to give some good results, but it can actually cause a lot of damage to your muscles and can even cause some more injuries in the long term.

- Make it a bit challenging—you should have some challenges that are with your workout. If the workout is too easy, you are not going to see some of the growth that you want. It shouldn't be so hard that you aren't able to complete the reps that you want, but you should have a bit of a struggle in the process and should make you work for it. With a bit of challenge, you are going to see that it is easier to work those muscles and to get the muscle growth that you want.

- Take some time off—you can't ask the muscles to workout strong each and every day. Some beginners make this mistake and assume that they are going to be going to the gym each day and spend hours there to get the results. This is going to work against you. You are going to end up exhausting the muscles, and they won't get stronger because you will not stick with the workout program for the long term. It can also result in some injuries at the same time. If you do need to do something on your rest day, do a light cardio such as walking or jogging to keep the muscles loose and ready to go.

- Eat a healthy diet—if you want to see some of the best results, you will need to make sure that you are eating a diet that is healthy. It is hard to stay up with the workout program and to convince the muscles to work without failing if you don't provide the right nutrition that you need. You need to make sure that you are eating the lean meats, the good fruits and vegetables, and the whole grains while getting rid of all the bad stuff that is often found in the American diet. If you are able to do this along with the calorie burning of the intermittent fast, you are gong to see results faster than ever before.

- Stick with the routine—it is easy to take a day off and then have it turn into a few weeks without doing the muscle routine that you should be. Just sporadically going to the gym and working out is not going to give you the results that you are looking for, no matter how hard you are working on those gym days. You need to find the right workout program that you like and then stick with it for the long term. This is the only way that you are going to get the consistent results that you want so that the muscles can grow and you can avoid injury in the process.

Getting started on a new workout program, especially when you are looking to get that lean muscle or to build the bulk, can be really exciting. You will find that following some of the tips that are in this chapter is going to make it easier than before to get the results that you want, especially when you add in a healthy diet program, like intermittent fasting, that helps your body to burn off the extra fat and still get the nutrition that you need.

Conclusion

Say goodbye to the days of struggling and disappointment. Intermittent fasting makes the journey to weight loss, health, and fitness easy, enjoyable, and fun. Now that you understand how your body works, you will be able to make intermittent fasting work for you by choosing a method that suits you and your lifestyle. With intermittent fasting, you will be able to satisfy your cravings without sacrificing results. Now, healthy living will become a part of your life, rather than an added chore. Taking the time to learn about nutrition and intermittent fasting methods is a huge step, and now, you've already taken it! As you begin your journey, be sure to congratulate yourself on your accomplishments, no matter how big or small. Remember, change does not occur overnight, so be patient with your results, and most of all, with yourself.

Keep an open mind and keep your eyes peeled for emerging information about the body, nutrition, and intermittent fasting as it is discovered! Stay focused on your goals, and know that you are capable of achieving all of them.

Ketogenic Diet Meal Prep

Weight Loss Cookbook with Breakfast, Lunch, and Dinner Recipes

Introduction

This book contains proven steps and strategies on how to go on the keto diet and prepare delicious and nutritious keto meals.

Learn how the keto diet works and how you can get started on it. Find out which foods are keto-approved and how to create meal plans based on these guidelines. Most importantly, learn how to prepare a variety of keto breakfast, lunch, and dinner meals that are chock full of the nutrients and energy that your body needs.

This book was written for anyone who wants to lose weight, manage type 2 diabetes, and reduce his or her risk of developing cancer and other debilitating diseases. It is also for anyone who is curious about the keto diet and would like to understand it as well as give it a try.

Get started on the keto diet now and transform your body into a high energy fat-burning machine!

Thanks again for downloading this book. I hope you enjoy it!

Chapter 1 - How to Get Started: Keto versus Normal Diets

The ketogenic diet, often called *keto* for short, is described as high in fat and low in carbohydrates. It was originally designed to help those with epilepsy cope with their medical condition, but studies later on revealed that the diet can also help reduce the risk of the development of type 2 diabetes, cancer, and Alzheimer's disease. This is because the keto diet can significantly reduce insulin and blood sugar levels.

To be on the keto diet, you need to significantly reduce your intake of carbohydrates and instead get your daily source of energy from fat. After approximately two weeks of being consistently on the keto diet, your body will eventually get into the state of *ketosis*. During this state, the body will start transforming the fat stores in the liver into ketones which will be then be used as its main source of energy.

The keto diet is completely unique from other diets because it is concentrated on the consumption of high amounts of fat. Normal diets, on the other hand, focus on deprivation of not just carbohydrates but also fat. This means you do not have to "starve" your body. In other words, you can still enjoy delicious and nutritious meals throughout the day.

The Types of Keto Diets

There are four main types of keto diets, each of which is designed to address specific needs. These are: the Standard Ketogenic Diet (SKD), the High-Protein Ketogenic Diet, the Cyclical Ketogenic Diet (CKD), and the Targeted Ketogenic Diet (TKD).

- **Standard Ketogenic Diet** - this type of keto diet is characterized as extremely low in carbohydrates (approximately 5 percent), regular in protein (approximately 20 percent), and high in fat (approximately 75 percent). This ratio is to be followed in every meal with no exceptions.

- **High-Protein Ketogenic Diet** - while this type of keto diet is almost the same as the SKD; the big difference is in the increased protein intake. Hence, the ratio for this diet should be 5 percent carbs, 35 percent protein, and 60 percent fat.

- **Cyclical Ketogenic Diet** - this type of keto diet is a cyclic system between a primarily keto diet with brief high carb feeding intervals. The common practice would be five days on the keto diet followed by two days on the high carb diet before going right back to the keto diet.

- **Targeted Ketogenic Diet** - this is a special type of keto diet that is meant for those who work out regularly, especially among athletes. Specifically, it involves adding some carbohydrates before each intensive workout.

It is imperative that you consult your doctor before following the keto diet because the state of ketosis does have detrimental effects on certain people, especially those who are at risk of heart attacks, stroke, atherosclerosis, and other cardiovascular diseases.

It is equally important to work with a licensed fitness expert if you plan to follow the keto diet with a sound workout program. For those who wish to follow it for weight loss, then it is best to consult a dietitian in order to determine your daily caloric and nutritional needs and to match them with the appropriate meal plans.

Common Myths Regarding the Keto Diet

It is only natural to be skeptical of a diet, especially one that is controversial due to the fact that it highly encourages fat consumption. To help debunk the myths and clear the fog, below is a list of the true answers to the common concerns with regard to the keto diet:

Myth #1: You can' t build muscles on the keto diet.
This one is false because you definitely can build muscles with the keto diet. However, this can only be effectively achieved with the Cyclical or Targeted Ketogenic Diet types than with the Standard or High-Protein types.

Myth #2: You will frequently feel fatigued when you are following the keto diet regularly.
Partly false, because if this occurs then your body may not be properly transforming your fat stores into ketones that should serve as your main source of energy. If you experience fatigue even after two weeks into the keto diet, then you should do your best to eliminate carb intake and consult your physician regarding supplements such as MCT oil.

Myth #3: I can no longer eat carbs for the rest of my life when I' m on the keto diet.
This one is false, especially if you are exercising regularly (see the Cyclical or Targeted Ketogenic Diets). However, it is imperative that you completely eliminate carbs within the first 60 to 90 days into the keto diet. After that, you may eat small amounts of healthy sources of complex carbohydrates during special events.

Myth #4: I will experience muscle mass loss with the keto diet.
Partially true. However, take note that *any* type of diet that eliminates a macro nutrient (in this case, carbohydrates) will trigger muscle mass loss. If your goal is to increase muscle mass, then you should choose the Cyclical or Targeted Keto diets.

Myth #5: If I follow the keto diet, I will suffer from mild halitosis (or bad breath).
This is a normal side effect of ketosis, but it is a minor setback that can easily be addressed if you drink mint tea or lemon water regularly, or if you chew sugar-free gum.

Myth #6: The keto diet will cause my pee to smell fruity.
This is another side effect of ketosis and should not be something of concern, unless your urine is of an unusual color.

Myth #7: Ketosis is life-threatening and not worth the health benefits of the keto diet.
False. Ketosis is often confused with ketoacidosis, which is a condition that takes place when a person with diabetes does not do anything to control his or her condition. Ketosis, on the other hand, is natural. Nevertheless, consult your doctor before starting the keto diet for safety reasons.

How to Get Started on the Keto Diet

Now that you have a general idea of what the keto diet is all about and what to expect from it, you can now put your knowledge into action. Here are the steps on how to get started:

Step 1: Consult a Health Professional to determine whether or not you can start the keto diet.

Step 2: Determine which type of keto diet is ideal for you based on your health and fitness goals.

Step 3: Design a meal plan and collect recipes that are sustainable for you depending on your lifestyle and personal preferences.

Step 4: Clean out your kitchen to get rid of any foods that you should avoid while on the keto diet.

Step 5: Create a grocery list of the food items you need for your meal plan.

Step 6: Research online on where to purchase the best quality and most affordable food items in your grocery list.

Step 7: Shop in bulk for your food items.

Step 8: Prepare your keto meals.

Keep in mind that you will need to make a conscious effort in sticking to your keto diet. Ideally, you should incorporate a regular workout regimen as well. This will require loads of self-discipline, especially if you have gotten so used to the conventional, carb-filled diet.

Be determined and constantly motivated, and eventually the keto diet will become second nature to you. Soon enough, you are well on your way to becoming strong, lean and full of energy.

Chapter 2 - The Ketogenic Diet Food List

The Ketogenic diet is all about fresh, natural ingredients. You should choose only the best produce that your budget can afford so that you can get the most amount of nutrients from each serving.

That being said, here is the comprehensive list of foods that you should stock up on when following the keto diet:

Healthy fats and oil
Fat is the primary source of energy in the keto diet, therefore most of your daily caloric needs should be from fats. Healthy fats should be in the form of Omega-3 fatty acids, such as from wild-caught salmon, tuna, and other fatty fish. If fish is not a good option for you, then you should consider taking fish oil supplements. Omega-6 fatty acids are also important in the keto diet. You can get them from eggs, nuts, and poultry. Make sure to choose the organic, whole foods kind.

Monounsaturated fats or the "good" fats take center-stage here. You can get them from olive oil, avocados and nuts. Choose the certified high quality "cold pressed" oils to ensure that you are regularly feeding your body with the right kind of fat.

Saturated fat is not considered a bad thing in the keto diet just as long as they come from organic sources, such as grass-fed butter and organic meat.

In a nutshell, you should stock up on the following healthy sources of fats and oil:

- Monounsaturated fats such as olives or olive oil, avocadoes and avocado oil, and macadamia nuts or macadamia oil.

- Polyunsaturated omega-3 sources, such as fatty fish and sea food.

- Saturated fat such as coconut oil and organic red meat (beef tallow, chicken fat, and non-hydrogenated lard).

Avoid at all costs anything that is hydrogenated and partially hydrogenated as these contain trans fats, or the most life-threatening fats that are linked to coronary heart disease.

Reduce consumption of inflammatory Omega-6 sources, particularly in the form of sunflower oil and corn oil.

Organic Meats

Protein is important in the human diet and you therefore should consume some, but it should be eaten in moderation in the keto diet. You should get your protein from certified organic sources that are locally produced and abundantly available in your area. This will ensure that you are feeding your body right and nourishing your muscles appropriately for optimum muscle mass gain.

By choosing local, organic and unprocessed meats, you are also significantly reducing your risk of consuming unhealthy hormones, additives, and other toxic substances that are linked to cancer and other debilitating diseases.

Here is a list of the different sources of protein to consider in the keto diet:

- Wild-caught fatty fish such as cod, flounder, mackerel, salmon, halibut, tuna, snapper, trout.
  If possible, purchase the fish fresh from the fisherman's wharf. Then, chop them into appropriate serving sizes, salt them, and pack them in your freezer to extend their shelf life for up to several weeks. Make sure to rinse off the sodium before cooking.

- Wild-caught shellfish such as crab, oysters, mussels, squid, scallops, and lobster.

These should also be bought fresh from the fisherman
' s wharf and stored in the same way as fish.

- Free-range (organic) eggs.

It is much better to find a local source such as a nearby
farmer' s market or a local farmer to obtain your eggs
instead of buying the pre-packaged ones at the
supermarket.

- Poultry such as duck, chicken, turkey, quail, and
  pheasant.

Opt for free-range fowls from ethical local farmers
instead of from industrially produced ones as the
former have higher quality protein and fat.

- Meat such as beef, lamb, goat, pork and wild game.
  Choose grass-fed, pastured organic meat whenever
  possible because these contain significantly higher
  levels of fatty acid that your body will need.

Dairy Products

Full fat, organic milk products are ideal in the keto
diet. This includes cheeses and creams. Some of the most
commonly used milk products are:

- Buttermilk
- Cheddar cheese
- Colby cheese
- Cream cheese
- Feta cheese
- Monterey Jack cheese
- Mozzarella cheese
- Swiss cheese
- Heavy cream
- Sour cream
- Whole milk

Vegetables

Your main source of nutrients in the keto diet should come from leafy greens and other vegetables. Ideally, these should be locally produced, organic, and in-season to ensure freshness, optimum nutritional value, and of course, cheaper prices.

Here is a list of vegetables that are low in carbohydrates. If any of these are too expensive or unavailable in your area, search online or call your local nutrition center to identify the best alternatives.

- Kale
- Spinach

- Bok choy
- Chard
- Chives
- Endive
- Radicchio
- Kohlrabi
- Bamboo shoots
- Lettuce
- Cabbage
- Asparagus
- Broccoli
- Carrots
- Cauliflower
- Celery
- Cucumber
- Garlic
- Green beans
- Mushrooms
- Onion
- Bell pepper
- Shallots
- Snow peas
- Spinach
- Squash (such as acorn, butternut, and spaghetti)

Nuts and Seeds

Plenty of nuts and seeds are used in the keto diet and the generally preferred way to prepare them is through roasting. Take note that peanuts are legumes and should be consumed in small amounts in the keto diet.

Here is a list of the nuts and seeds commonly consumed when you are on the keto diet:

- Almonds
- Cashews
- Chestnuts
- Chia seeds
- Coconuts
- Flaxseeds
- Hazelnuts
- Macadamia nuts
- Pecans
- Pistachios
- Pumpkin seeds
- Sesame seeds
- Walnuts

Beverages and Sweetener

It is important to drink lots of water each day, especially when you are on the keto diet. This is because the diet is naturally diuretic, which means you will need to visit the toilet regularly. If you are not careful, you could also end up getting dehydrated. Keep a container full of fresh drinking water with you at all times and stay hydrated.

Aside from water, you can also enjoy black coffee and herbal tea. Avoid everything else except for keto-approved smoothies. If you have to sweeten your drinks or food, then use liquid stevia.

Chapter 3 - Create Your Own Keto Meal Plan

Your personalized keto meal plan should be more than just a list of the foods that you are supposed to eat each day. Rather, it also serves as your guide so that you will not stray from or cheat on your diet. Preparing meal plans ahead of time will help you save a lot of time, money and effort put into preparing your own keto meals at home. That being said, here are the steps on how you can create your own keto meal plan:

Step 1: Determine how many calories your body needs in a day.

There are five main factors that determine how many calories your body needs each day in order to function properly, and these are your height, weight, age, sex, and activity level. It is important to take note of these before going online and finding an online "daily caloric needs" calculator.

For example, if you are a 27 year old woman who weighs 128 pounds and is 5 feet 1 inch tall and does no exercise at all, then the online calculator will reveal that you need about 1500 calories a day to maintain your current weight. If your goal is to lose weight, then you need to consume no more than 1000 to 1200 calories per day.

If you would rather calculate manually, then follow this formula to determine your basic metabolic rate:

For men: 66.5 + (13.75 x weight in kilograms) + (5.003 x height in centimeters) - (6.755 x age in years)

For women: 655.1 + (4.35 x weight in pounds) + (4.7 x height in inches) - (4.7 x age in years)

For instance, if you are a 28 year old man who weighs 77 kilograms and is 177.8 centimeters tall, then you should calculate your BMR this way:
66.5 + (13.75 x 77) + (5.003 x 177.8) - (6.755 x 28) = 1825.64

This means you need to consume 1825.64 calories per day to maintain your weight, less 200 or so calories to lose weight and the other way around to gain weight.

Take note that you need to burn 3500 calories to lose one pound and vice versa.

Step 2: Identify the times when you can have meals.

Ideally, you should eat three regular meals and three small meals per day, especially when you are on the keto diet. To be more specific, your everyday meal plan should consist of:

- 1 Breakfast
- 1 Morning Snack
- 1 Lunch
- 1 Afternoon Snack
- 1 Dinner
- 1 Evening Snack

Each meal should be about 3 to 4 hours apart so that you will avoid "feeling" hungry, which in turn will make you more likely to succumb to your food cravings. It is important to stick to this healthy eating habit and you can make it easier for yourself by setting timers to remind you that it is time to eat.

For example, you can set a timer at 7:30 am for breakfast, 10:30 am for your morning snack, 1:30 pm for lunch, 4:30 pm for your afternoon snack, 7:30 pm for dinner, and 10:30 pm for evening snack (if necessary).

Take note that you will need to distribute your ideal daily recommended number of calories among your meals so that you are sure to hit your health goals.

Step 3: Decide on how you should prepare your meals.

Your meal plan should be more than just a list of the food you need to eat per mealtime; it should also be your guide in preparing your food. More often than not, you would not have the luxury of time to prepare elaborate meals during busy work days so the next best strategy is to make your meals ahead of time. Doing so will keep you stress-free and on track with regard to your keto diet. Of course, if you do have the time and energy to cook before each mealtime then this is an ideal setup.

To prepare your meals ahead of time, you will need to choose a specific time of the week for buying all of your ingredients in bulk and another time for cooking them all and storing them appropriately in the freezer or refrigerator. Usually, this takes place on a Sunday afternoon.

The first thing you need to do is choose recipes for your meals. A highly practical guide for super busy individuals would be as three sets of recipes: one for Monday, Wednesday, and Friday, one for Tuesday, Saturday, and one for Thursday and Sunday.

Here is an example of three sets of meal plans following the Standard Keto Diet and using the recipes in the succeeding chapters:

Set 1 for Monday, Wednesday and Friday (to be stored in separate containers in the refrigerator except for the smoothies)

Breakfast and Morning Snack: Keto Espresso Smoothie, Coconut Banana Raisin Pancakes (3 servings)

Lunch and Afternoon Snack: Baked Cheesy Chicken Balls, Grilled Radicchio with Balsamic Vinaigrette (3 servings)
Dinner and Evening Snack: Poblano Peppers Stuffed with Pork and Cheese, Buttered Spinach with Shallots and Bacon (3 servings)

Set 2 for Tuesday and Saturday (to be stored in separate containers in the freezer)

Breakfast and Morning Snack: Avocado and Raspberry Smoothie, Cheddar Flapjacks (2 servings)

Lunch and Afternoon Snack: Tex Mex Turkey Salad, Cheesy Broccoli (2 servings)

Dinner and Evening Snack: Stewed Beef and Mushrooms, Avocado and Cucumber Salad (2 servings)

Set 3 for Thursday and Sunday (to be stored in separate containers in the freezer)

Breakfast and Morning Snack: Coconut Spice Smoothie, Bacon Avocado Breakfast Muffins (2 servings)

Lunch and Afternoon Snack: Chicken Barbecue Stew, Cheddar Broccoli Biscuits (2 servings)

Dinner and Evening Snack: Cheesy Tuna and Cauliflower Casserole, Savory Roasted Spaghetti Squash with Kale (2 servings)

With a meal plan system such as this, all you will need to do for the rest of the week is reheat and serve. Continue to adjust your meal plan based on your personal schedule, the types of food you want to eat while on the keto diet, and whatever is available on the market. Make it a habit to prepare your own keto meals and keep things simple and streamlined so that meal planning becomes a sustainable part of your lifestyle.

Chapter 4 - Breakfast Recipes

Get your metabolism revved up at the start of the day by enjoying a healthy, delicious ketogenic breakfast meal. Keto breakfast dishes are high in healthy fats, fiber, lean protein and lots of nutrients from herbs and other fresh ingredients. Serve yours with a hot cup of black coffee or tea, or even just a tall, cold glass of lemon water. Adding just a bit of sliced fruit on the side won' t hurt either.

The following keto breakfast recipes can be prepared during the previous night and then refrigerated to be reheated and served for breakfast the following day. Of course, fresh is always best so find the time to wake up just a bit earlier to prepare breakfast for it is truly worth the effort.

Breakfast Meals

Herb and Mushroom Egg Scramble

Makes 4 servings

Ingredients:

- 1 Tbsp olive oil
- 4 large organic eggs
- 2 cups sliced fresh mushrooms
- 1 small onion, minced
- 5 oz grated cheddar cheese
- 2 Tbsp chopped fresh or 2 tsp dried flat leaf parsley
- 2 Tbsp chopped fresh or 2 tsp dried dill
- ½ Tbsp chopped fresh or ½ tsp dried thyme
- Sea salt
- Freshly ground black pepper

Procedure:
Beat the eggs and season with salt and pepper. Set aside
Place a cast iron skillet over medium high flame and heat through. Once hot, add half the olive oil and reduce to medium flame.

Add the onion and mushroom, then sauté until tender. Stir in the herbs and sauté for 1 minute or until fragrant and wilted, if using fresh. Transfer to a plate and set aside.
Wipe the skillet to clean it. Heat what's left of remaining olive oil. Then add the beaten eggs and scramble until halfway done.

Return the mushroom and herb mixture into the skillet and mix well with the scrambled egg. Cook until the egg is done to a desired consistency.

Transfer to a plate and serve right away.

Coconut Banana Raisin Pancakes

Makes 3 servings

Ingredients:
- 3 large organic eggs
- ¼ cup coconut flour
- 1 Tbsp coconut milk
- 1 Tbsp ground cinnamon
- ¼ tsp ground nutmeg
- ¼ tsp baking soda
- 1 cup raisins
- 2 small ripe bananas, mashed
- Nonstick cooking spray
- Grass-fed butter

Procedure:
Sift the flour, cinnamon, nutmeg, and baking soda in a bowl.
Set aside.

Whisk the eggs, mashed banana, and milk together, then mix
in the flour mixture until thoroughly incorporated.

Place a pancake griddle over medium high flame and lightly
coat with nonstick cooking spray, if needed.

Pour a quarter cup of the batter on the griddle and sprinkle
some raisins on top.

Cook for 1 to 2 minutes per side, or until firm. Repeat with the rest of the batter.

Best served warm with butter.

Cheddar Flapjacks

Makes 4 servings

Ingredients:
- 2 Tbsp olive oil
- 2 large egg whites
- ¼ cup water
- 1 cup almond flour
- ½ tsp baking powder
- 2 oz grated cheddar cheese
- 1 garlic clove, minced
- ½ Tbsp chopped green onion
- Grass-fed butter
- Nonstick cooking spray

Procedure:
Whisk the egg whites and water until thoroughly combined. Then, fold in the cheese, almond flour, baking powder, garlic, and green onion.

Gradually pour in the olive oil as you mix until the batter is well incorporated.

Place a pancake griddle over medium high flame and lightly coat with nonstick cooking spray, if needed.

Pour a quarter cup of the batter on the griddle and cook for 1 to 2 minutes per side, or until firm. Repeat with the rest of the batter.

Best served warm with butter.

Bacon Avocado Breakfast Muffins
Makes 24 servings

Ingredients:
- 8 large organic eggs
- 3 Tbsp freshly squeezed lemon juice
- 4 avocados, pitted and peeled
- 3 cups coconut milk
- 10 slices unprocessed bacon
- 1 cup almond flour
- ½ cup ground flaxseeds
- 3 Tbsp ground psyllium husks
- 9 oz Colby Jack cheese

- 2 tsp minced garlic
- 2 tsp dried cilantro
- 2 tsp dried chives
- ½ tsp red chili flakes
- 2 tsp baking powder
- 6 spring onions, minced
- Sea salt
- Freshly ground black pepper

Procedure:
Set the oven to 350 degrees F. Lightly grease 24 muffin tins with butter and set aside.

Place a cast iron skillet over medium high flame and heat through. Add the bacon and cook until crisp. Transfer to a plate lined with paper towels and set aside.

Combine the almond flour with the ground flaxseeds, psyllium husks, dried spices, baking powder and chili flakes.

Combine the avocado with the eggs, lemon juice and coconut milk. Mash well until thoroughly incorporated.

Combine the almond flour mixture with the avocado mixture until well incorporated. Fold in the cheese, garlic, and green onion. Season to taste with salt and pepper.

Divide the mixture among the muffin tins, then bake for 25 minutes, or until muffins are firm and golden brown.

Serve warm. Muffins can be stored in the freezer for up to 3 weeks and reheated in the broiler before serving.

Bacon Ricotta Breakfast Muffins

Makes 24 servings

Ingredients:
- 10 slices unprocessed bacon
- 2 cups grated Parmesan cheese
- 2 lb ricotta cheese
- 20 oz baby spinach, washed and drained thoroughly
- 1 cup plain yogurt
- 4 large eggs
- 4 oz chopped pine nuts
- Sea salt
- Freshly ground black pepper
- Grass-fed butter

Procedure:
Set the oven to 350 degrees F. Lightly grease 24 muffin tins with butter and set aside.

Boil salted water in a saucepan, then blanch the baby spinach for 30 seconds. Drain thoroughly, then mince and set aside.

Mince the bacon and place in a bowl. Fold in the spinach, cheeses, yogurt, and eggs. Season with a bit of salt and pepper, then pour the batter into the prepared muffin tins.

Top with pine nuts, then bake for 30 minutes, or until the muffins are firm and tops are golden brown.

Serve warm. Muffins can be stored in the freezer for up to 3 weeks and reheated in the broiler before serving.

Creamy Keto Porridge

Makes 4 servings

Ingredients:
- ½ cup unsweetened shredded coconut
- 2 Tbsp oat bran
- 2 Tbsp ground flaxseeds
- 1 tsp ground cinnamon
- 1 cup heavy cream
- 2 cups water
- Sea salt
- 1 Tbsp grass-fed butter

Procedure:

Combine the shredded coconut, oat bran and flaxseed meal in a saucepan, then stir in the cinnamon, heavy cream, water, and a pinch of salt.

Place over medium low flame and bring to a boil. Once boiling, immediately turn off the heat and stir.

Divide the mixture among four bowls. Let stand for 5 minutes, or until slightly thickened. Add a quarter tablespoon of butter on top of each serving, then serve warm.

Double Cheese Waffles

Makes 6 servings

Ingredients:
- 1 ½ cups chopped cauliflower florets
- 1 cup grated mozzarella cheese
- ¼ cup grated Parmesan cheese
- 2 large organic eggs
- 1 Tbsp chopped fresh chives
- 1 tsp onion powder
- 1 tsp garlic powder
- ½ tsp freshly ground black pepper

- Sea salt
- Grass-fed butter

Procedure:
Place the cauliflower florets in a food processor and pulse until crumbly. Transfer to a mixing bowl.

Fold the cheeses, eggs, chives, onion and garlic powders, black pepper, and a pinch of salt into the crumbled cauliflower. Mix very well.

Prepare the waffle maker based on manufacturer's instructions.

Pour just enough of the batter to fill the waffle maker, then cook for approximately 5 minutes or more.

Transfer to a plate and serve with butter.

Waffles can be made the previous night; simply refrigerate and reheat in the waffle maker the next morning.

Breakfast Smoothies

Keto Espresso Smoothie

Makes 2 servings

Ingredients:
- 2 scoops protein powder, no carbs
- 2 espresso shots
- ½ cup full fat Greek yogurt
- 2 cups ice cubes
- Cinnamon
- Liquid stevia

Procedure:
Pour the espresso, yogurt, protein powder, and ice cubes into a high power blender. Cover the blender, and then blend on high until smooth.

Add cinnamon and liquid stevia to taste, and then blend again. Pour into a tall glass and consume right away.

Avocado and Raspberry Smoothie

Makes 1 serving

Ingredients:
- ½ cup vanilla almond milk
- ½ cup diced avocado
- ½ Tbsp heavy cream
- ½ scoop protein powder, no carb
- 2 Tbsp frozen raspberries
- Liquid stevia

Procedure:
Combine the almond milk, avocado, heavy cream, and protein powder in a high power blender. Cover the blender, then blend on high until smooth.

Add the frozen raspberries and pulse until smooth with bits of raspberries still intact. Sweeten to taste with liquid stevia and blend again.

Pour into a tall glass and consume right away.

Green Blueberry Yogurt Smoothie

Makes 2 servings

Ingredients:

- 4 cups baby spinach leaves
- 1 cup full fat Greek yogurt
- 1 cup frozen blueberries
- 2 cups ice cubes
- 3 Tbsp coconut oil
- 2 Tbsp chia seeds

Procedure:

Pour the yogurt, ice cubes, coconut oil, chia seeds, and spinach leaves into a high power blender. Cover the blender, then blend on high until smooth.

Add the blueberries and pulse until smooth, with bits of blueberries still intact. Pour into a tall glass and consume right away.

Coconut Spice Smoothie

Makes 1 serving

Ingredients:
- ½ cup coconut milk
- 2 Tbsp unsweetened shredded coconut
- 1 Tbsp almond butter
- ½ Tbsp ground flaxseeds
- ½ Tbsp pure vanilla extract
- ½ tsp ground cinnamon
- ½ tsp ground ginger
- 3 ice cubes

Procedure:
Pour the coconut milk, almond butter, ground flaxseeds, vanilla extract, spices, and ice cubes in the blender.

Cover the blender, then blend on high until smooth. Pour into a tall glass and consume right away.

Spiced Sweet Potato Smoothie

Makes 2 servings

Ingredients:
- 2 small sweet potatoes, peeled, boiled, and cubed
- 1 ½ cups vanilla almond milk
- ¼ cup avocado
- 2 scoops protein powder, no carb
- 2 tsp pure vanilla extract
- 1 tsp ground cinnamon
- ½ tsp ground nutmeg
- ½ tsp ground allspice

Procedure:
Place the sweet potato into the blender, then add the almond milk, avocado, protein powder, vanilla extract, and spices.

Cover the blender, then blend on high until smooth. Pour into a tall glass and consume right away.

Peanut Butter Smoothie

Makes 1 serving

Ingredients:
- ½ cup vanilla almond milk
- ½ cup ice cubes
- ¼ cup coconut milk
- 1 Tbsp smooth peanut butter, natural
- ½ tsp pure vanilla extract
- Liquid stevia

Procedure:
Pour the almond milk, coconut milk, ice cubes, vanilla extract, and peanut butter in a high power blender.
Cover the blender, then blend on high until smooth. Sweeten to taste with liquid stevia, then blend again to combine.

Pour into a tall glass and consume right away.

Buttered Pumpkin Spice Latte

Makes 2 servings

Ingredients:
- 1 cup brewed coffee
- 4 Tbsp pureed pumpkin
- 2 Tbsp almond milk
- 2 Tbsp grass-fed butter
- ½ tsp pumpkin pie spice
- Liquid stevia

Procedure:
Combine the almond milk, brewed coffee, butter, pureed pumpkin, and pumpkin pie spice in a high power blender. Cover the blender, then blend on high until smooth.

Sweeten to taste with liquid stevia and blend again. Pour into a tall glass and consume right away.

Chapter 5 - Lunch Recipes

Keto lunch dishes are highly satisfying and full of energy and nutrients from fresh ingredients. Choose only the best organic ingredients from your local farmer's market and do not hesitate to opt for fresher, locally produced alternatives instead of the usual ingredients listed. The key to a healthy keto diet is in the quality of the produce, after all.

Follow any of these healthy keto lunch recipes to prepare lunch meals ahead of time. Store the meals in airtight lunch boxes and refrigerate. That way, all you will have to do later on is reheat in the microwave or enjoy chilled. It helps to pack a thermos full of hot green tea to not only make your lunch more special, but also to help boost your metabolism and maximize your body's fat-burning power.

Main Course Recipes

Baked Cheesy Chicken Balls

Makes 12 servings

Ingredients:

- ½ lb ground chicken breast
- ½ cup almond flour
- ½ cup tomato sauce
- ¼ cup grated Parmesan cheese
- 1.5 oz fresh mozzarella cheese
- ¼ cup full cream milk
- ½ tsp sea salt
- ¼ tsp dried oregano
- Freshly ground black pepper
- Nonstick cooking spray

Procedure:

Set the oven to 350 degrees F. Lightly coat a baking dish with nonstick cooking spray and set aside.

Combine the parmesan, milk, salt, oregano, and half the almond flour in a bowl. Mix well, and then fold in the ground chicken. Mix until well incorporated.

Divide the mixture into 12 equal sized balls and dredge each in the remaining flour.

Arrange the chicken balls on the prepared baking dish, and then bake for 20 minutes, turning the balls once halfway through the cooking time.

Pour the tomato sauce over the baked chicken balls, and then add the mozzarella cheese on top.

Bake again for 12 minutes, or until the mozzarella is melted. Best served warm with a fresh green salad.

Greek Tuna Salad

Makes 6 servings

Ingredients:

- 15 oz BPA-free canned white albacore tuna in oil, drained
- ¾ cup extra virgin olive oil
- 1 ½ cups crumbled feta cheese
- 1/3 cup chopped green olives
- 1/3 cup chopped fresh flat leaf parsley
- ¾ cup diced roasted red bell peppers
- 1 ½ Tbsp freshly squeezed lemon juice
- 1 ½ Tbsp chopped capers
- 3 cups endive leaves
- Sea salt
- Freshly ground black pepper

Procedure:
Arrange the endive leaves on a serving plate and set aside. Crumble the tuna with clean hands, then mix in the olive oil, feta cheese, green olives, lemon juice, capers, parsley, and roasted red bell peppers. Mix well.

Season to taste with salt and pepper, then spoon the mixture on top of the bed of endive leaves. Serve right away.

Chicken Barbecue Stew

Makes 4 servings

Ingredients:
- 2 Tbsp olive oil
- 4 chicken thighs
- 2 cups chicken stock, low sodium
- 2 cups beef stock, low sodium
- 3 tsp chili powder
- Sea salt
- Freshly ground black pepper

For the Barbecue Sauce:
- 1/3 cup tomato sauce
- 1/3 cup tomato paste
- 3 Tbsp Dijon mustard
- 1 ½ tsp low sodium soy sauce
- 1 ½ Tbsp Tabasco sauce
- 3 tsp liquid smoke
- 1 ½ tsp Worcestershire sauce
- 2 tsp garlic powder
- 1 ½ tsp chili powder
- 1 ½ tsp garlic powder
- 1 ½ tsp red chili flakes
- 1 ½ tsp cumin
- 1/3 cup grass-fed butter

Procedure:

Mix together all the ingredients for the barbecue sauce, then set aside.

Set the oven to 400 degrees F. Line a baking sheet with aluminum foil and set aside.
Remove the chicken meat from the bones, then season the meat with chili powder.

Lay the chicken meat on the prepared baking sheet and bake for 45 minutes.

Place a stockpot over medium high flame and heat through. Once hot, add the olive oil and swirl to coat.

Sauté the chicken bones for 5 minutes, then stir in the chicken and beef stocks.

Once the chicken meat is cooked, remove the skin and add the roasted chicken meat to the pot. Mix well until combined.

Stir in the barbecue sauce and mix well. Let simmer for 15 minutes, then ladle into soup bowls and serve right away with a fresh green salad.

Avocado Beef Patties

Makes 2 servings

Ingredients:
- ½ lb lean organic ground beef
- 1 small avocado, pitted and peeled
- ¼ Tbsp freshly squeezed lemon juice
- 2 slices yellow cheddar cheese, 1 oz each
- 1 tomato, diced
- 1 small onion, sliced into thin rings
- 4 romaine or iceberg lettuce leaves
- Sea salt
- Freshly ground black pepper

Procedure:
Lay the lettuce leaves on two serving dishes and set aside. Divide the ground beef into two patties. Make compact, then season with salt and pepper.

Prepare the stovetop grill. Grill the beef patties for 5 to 8 minutes per side or until cooked through.

Lay a patty over each bed of lettuce.

Slice the avocado into thin pieces. Sprinkle the lemon juice over the sliced avocado to prevent them from browning.

Lay the sliced avocado on top of the burger patties, then add the chopped garlic and onion rings on top. Serve right away with yellow mustard, if desired.

Oriental Style Chicken Salad

Makes 4 servings

Ingredients:
- 4 cups torn lettuce
- 2 ½ cups shredded cooked chicken
- 4 slices unprocessed bacon
- 1 ½ cups shredded cabbage
- 3 Tbsp diced canned water chestnuts
- 3 Tbsp shredded carrot
- 5 green onions, chopped
- 1/3 cup slivered almonds
- 1 ½ Tbsp sesame seeds
- ¾ Tbsp grass-fed butter

For the Sesame Dressing:
- 3 Tbsp low sodium soy sauce
- 2 Tbsp rice vinegar
- 1 Tbsp dark sesame oil
- 1 garlic clove, crushed
- 2 tsp freshly squeezed lemon juice
- 1/3 tsp freshly ground black pepper

Procedure:

Combine all the ingredients for the dressing in a bowl, then set aside.

Combine the lettuce, cabbage, carrot, chestnuts, and green onion. Refrigerate until ready to serve.

Place a cast iron skillet over medium high flame and cook the bacon to a crisp. Set aside on a plate lined with paper towels.

In the same skillet, cook the almonds, sesame seeds, and butter until golden brown. Transfer to a plate.

Take the vegetables out of the refrigerator, then add the dressing and almond and sesame seed mixture. Toss well to combine.

Divide among four plates and add the chicken on top, followed by the bacon. Serve chilled or warm.

Pork and Mushroom Meatballs

Makes 2 servings

Ingredients:
- ¾ lb organic lean ground pork
- ½ cup minced fresh mushrooms, any kind
- ½ Tbsp low sodium soy sauce

- 1 Tbsp chopped green onion
- ¼ tsp sesame oil
- 1 small organic egg
- 1/8 tsp garlic powder
- ¼ tsp sea salt
- 1/8 tsp freshly ground black pepper

Procedure:
Place the ground pork in a bowl, and then fold in the minced mushrooms. Add the soy sauce, salt, pepper, garlic powder, green onion, egg, and sesame oil.

Mix well, and then form into small inch sized balls.

Boil water in a saucepan over medium high flame, and then add the meatballs. Cover and simmer over medium flame for about 10 minutes, or until the meatballs are completely cooked.

Transfer the meatballs to a bowl using a slotted spoon then serve warm, preferably with a green salad.

Tex Mex Turkey Salad

Makes 2 servings

Ingredients:

- 1 cup cooked diced turkey
- 2 cups chopped cauliflower florets
- 1 small red bell pepper, seeded and diced
- 1 small red onion, diced
- 2 Tbsp chopped canned green chilies
- 3 oz Monterey Jack cheese, cubed
- 2 Tbsp chopped black olives
- 3 Tbsp mayonnaise
- ½ Tbsp white wine vinegar
- ¾ tsp freshly squeezed lime juice
- ½ tsp chili powder
- ¼ tsp ground cumin
- ¼ tsp dried oregano
- 2 Tbsp chopped fresh cilantro

Procedure:

Combine the mayonnaise, oregano, chili powder, cumin, vinegar, and lime juice in a bowl. Refrigerate until ready to serve.

Steam the cauliflower florets in a bowl of water in the microwave or in a steamer basket over boiling water for 5 minutes, or until tender.

Drain the cauliflower, then transfer to a bowl and allow to cool slightly. Add the bell pepper, red onion, green chilies, black olives, cooked diced turkey, and cubed cheese. Toss well to combine.

Add the dressing and fold gently to coat. Garnish with fresh cilantro, then serve.

Side Dish or Snack Recipes

Grilled Radicchio with Balsamic Vinaigrette

Makes 9 servings

Ingredients:
- 2 radicchios, sliced into thin wedges
- 1 ½ Tbsp balsamic vinegar
- 1 ½ Tbsp extra virgin olive oil
- Sea salt

Procedure:
Set the broiler to high heat.

Whisk together the balsamic vinegar, olive oil, and a pinch of sea salt. Mix well, then add the radicchio wedges and toss well to coat.

Spread the radicchio wedges on the broiler pan, then broil for 5 minutes per side, or until grilled tightly.

Set on a cooling rack and allow to cool slightly, then store in a glass bowl. Cover and serve right away, or refrigerate.

Cheesy Broccoli
Makes 6 servings

Ingredients:
- 3 cups chopped broccoli florets
- ¾ cup shredded sharp Cheddar cheese
- 1/3 cup heavy cream
- 1/3 Tbsp ranch dressing
- Sea salt
- Freshly ground black pepper

Procedure:
Set the oven to 375 degrees F.

Combine the ranch dressing, cheddar cheese, and heavy cream. Season to taste with salt and pepper, and then add the chopped broccoli. Mix well until combined.

144

Pour the mixture into the casserole dish, and then spread out. Bake for 20 to 30 minutes, or until the cheese is bubbly and the broccoli is fork tender.

Best served warm.

Cheddar Broccoli Biscuits

Makes 6 to 8 servings

Ingredients:
- ½ cup melted coconut oil, cooled
- 3 cups almond flour
- 8 cups chopped broccoli florets
- 4 large organic eggs
- 1 tsp apple cider vinegar
- 1 tsp baking soda
- 2 tsp garlic powder
- 2 tsp paprika
- 2 tsp sea salt
- 2 tsp freshly ground black pepper

Procedure:
Set the oven to 375 degrees F. Line a baking sheet with parchment paper and set aside.

Place the broccoli in a food processor and process until minced. Work in batches.

Combine the almond flour and spices in a mixing bowl, and then mix in the coconut oil, vinegar, and eggs. Mix well to form a dough.

Fold in the broccoli and Cheddar cheese, mixing well.

Divide the mixture into 24 balls, and then press the balls on the prepared baking sheet, leaving over an inch of space between each piece.

Bake for 5 minutes, then set on a cooling rack and allow to cool slightly. Serve right away or store in an airtight container.

Mashed Cauliflower and Turnip

Makes 4 servings

Ingredients:
- ½ lb chopped cauliflower
- ½ lb fresh turnips
- ¼ cup heavy cream
- ¼ cup grass-fed butter
- Sea salt

Procedure:
Place the turnips and cauliflower in a pot, then add enough water to cover them by an about two inches. Add a generous pinch of salt.

Place over high flame and bring to a boil. Boil for 12 minutes or until extra tender. Drain thoroughly, then return to the pot and add the heavy cream and butter.

Mash everything until smooth, then serve right away or transfer to an airtight container and refrigerate.

Baked Garlic Parmesan Cauliflower

Makes 3 servings

Ingredients:
- 3 cups chopped cauliflower florets
- 4 Tbsp grass-fed butter
- 3 Tbsp shredded Parmesan cheese
- 2 garlic cloves, minced
- Sea salt

Procedure:
Set the oven to 350 degrees F.

Combine the butter and garlic in a saucepan, then place over low flame. Heat until the garlic is golden. Set aside.

Spread the cauliflower on a rimmed baking sheet, then pour the garlic butter on top and add salt and Parmesan cheese.

Bake for 15 minutes, or until the cauliflower is crisp tender. Serve right away.

Basic Cauliflower Rice

Makes 4 servings

Ingredients:
- 1 small cauliflower head
- 3 Tbsp water
- Sea salt
- Freshly ground black pepper

Procedure:

Rinse the cauliflower thoroughly, then chop and place in a food processor. Process until grainy, similar to rice grains.

Transfer the cauliflower rice to a microwaveable bowl, then add a pinch of salt and pepper. Add the water, then microwave for 2 minutes or until tender, but still firm.

Adjust seasoning to taste, if needed, then serve or store in an airtight container.

Tomato, Olive and Mozzarella Salad

Makes 2 servings

Ingredients:
- 1 ½ cups cherry tomatoes, halved
- 1 ½ cups pitted kalamata olives
- 1 ½ cups torn mozzarella cheese

Procedure:
In a bowl, combine the tomatoes, olives, and mozzarella cheese.

Serve right away, or store in an airtight container and refrigerate until ready to serve.

Chapter 6 - Dinner Recipes

Dinner should be treated as a special occasion every night and not just to celebrate a certain event. When you take the time to savor and appreciate the flavors of your meals, you become more likely to choose healthy food. A simple change of ambiance such as lit candles and music in tune with the theme of your dinner will make a big difference.

Follow these keto dinner recipes to present delicious and nutrient-packed dishes that are sure to make you look forward to your evening meals all the time. You can even serve with a hot cup of herbal tea to make it all the more relaxing. And, just like the lunch recipes, these dinner recipes call for organic and fresh ingredients. Choose the highest quality that your budget can afford because sure enough, your body deserves only the best.

Main Course Recipes

Poblano Peppers Stuffed with Pork and Cheese

Makes 3 to 4 servings

Ingredients:
- ¾ cup olive oil
- 1 ½ lb organic lean ground pork
- 2 cups freshly grated cheddar cheese
- 4 large poblano peppers
- 1 ½ cups salsa, unsweetened
- 1 ½ tsp chili powder
- 1 ½ Tbsp ground flaxseeds

Procedure:
Set the oven to 425 degrees F.

Halve the peppers lengthwise, then scoop out the seeds. Rinse the peppers and set aside to drain on paper towels.

Place a cast iron skillet over high flame and heat through. Add the olive oil, then sauté the ground pork with the chili powder until pork is crumbly and browned.

Remove from heat and fold in 1 ½ cups of cheddar cheese. Mix well until the cheese is melted.

Pour the salsa into a baking dish.

Stuff the halved peppers with the pork and cheese mixture, then arrange them on the prepared baking dish, cut sides facing up.

Top the stuffed peppers with the remaining cheddar cheese.

Bake the stuffed peppers for 30 minutes, uncovered. Sprinkle the ground flaxseed on top, then serve warm.

Sea Bass and Spinach with Coconut Lemon Sauce

Makes 2 servings

Ingredients:

- 2 large sea bass fillets (or salmon or halibut)
- 4 cups fresh spinach
- ½ cup coconut milk
- 2 ½ Tbsp freshly squeezed lemon juice
- 2 Tbsp pine nuts
- 2 Tbsp chopped fresh flat leaf parsley
- 2 Tbsp grass-fed butter
- Sea salt

Procedure:
Season the fish fillets on both sides with sea salt, then set aside.

Rinse and drain the spinach thoroughly, then dry in a colander or salad spinner. Set aside.

Place a cast iron skillet over medium high flame and heat through. Add half the butter in the skillet and reduce to medium flame. Cook the fillets for 4 minutes per side or until golden brown.

In the meantime, place another skillet over medium flame and heat the remaining butter. Sauté the spinach until wilted, then stir in the pine nuts and sauté until lightly toasted.

Place a saucepan over low flame and add the coconut milk. Stir in the parsley and lemon juice. Cook until heated through; do not boil.
Spread the spinach on the serving plate, then add the fish fillets on top. Spoon the sauce over the fillets, then serve right away.

Stewed Beef and Mushrooms

Makes 2 servings

Ingredients:
- ¼ cup olive oil
- 25 grams grass-fed butter
- ½ lb cubed stew beef
- ½ quart bone or beef broth
- ½ lb sliced fresh mushrooms, any kind
- ¼ cup diced onion
- ½ Tbsp ground flaxseeds
- ½ tsp minced garlic
- ½ tsp dried thyme
- 1 bay leaf
- 2 Tbsp chopped fresh parsley
- Sea salt
- Freshly ground black pepper
-

Procedure:
Place a stock pot over medium high flame and heat through.
Add the olive oil and butter, then stir in the cubed beef. Cook
until browned all over.

Stir in the onion and mushrooms, then sauté until tender.
Stir in the garlic, bay leaf, thyme, and ground flaxseeds, then
stir in the broth.

Bring to a boil, then reduce to low flame and simmer for 1 hour or until the beef is extra tender.

Discard the bay leaf. If desired, remove the cubed beef and shred using two forks. Stir back into the stew followed by the parsley.

Ladle into soup bowls and serve piping hot.

Cheesy Tuna and Cauliflower Casserole
Makes 9 servings

Ingredients:
- 18 oz canned chunky tuna
- ¾ cup chopped celery
- 1 ½ large cauliflower heads
- ½ cup chopped green onion
- 3 small zucchini, scrubbed and sliced
- 3 cups shredded cheddar or Monterey Jack cheese
- 2 small tomatoes, chopped
- 1 cup sour cream
- ¾ cup mayonnaise
- 3 tsp yellow mustard
- ¾ tsp dried thyme
- Sea salt

- Freshly ground black pepper

Procedure:
Set the oven to 350 degrees F.

Drain the tuna, then crumble in a bowl and fold in the green onion and celery.

Chop the cauliflower, then place in a steamer basket and steam over a pot of boiling water for 5 minutes or until fork tender.

Combine the tuna with the steamed cauliflower and mix well.

In a separate bowl, combine the mayonnaise, sour cream, thyme, mustard, salt, and pepper. Pour the mixture over the tuna and cauliflower mixture, then combine everything well.

Pack the mixture into a casserole dish, then lay the sliced zucchini on top. Sprinkle the cheese on top, then bake for 40 minutes, or until the casserole is bubbly hot.

Top with chopped tomato, then serve warm.

Crusted Fish Fillets with Dilled Sauce

Makes 4 servings

Ingredients:
- 1 ½ lb white fish fillets, wild-caught
- 1 large organic egg
- 1 cup freshly grated Parmesan cheese
- 1/3 tsp chili powder
- ¾ tsp dried parsley
- 1 cup almond meal
- 3 Tbsp organic mayonnaise
- 1/3 tsp sea salt
- Freshly ground black pepper
- Coconut oil

For the Dilled Sauce:
- 2/3 cup organic mayonnaise
- 2/3 cup sour cream
- 3 Tbsp chopped fresh dill
- 2 Tbsp chopped capers, drained
- 3 tsp freshly squeezed lemon juice
- Optional: 3 dill pickles, diced

Procedure:
Combine all the ingredients for the dilled sauce in a bowl, then cover and refrigerate until ready to serve.

In a shallow bowl, combine the Parmesan cheese, almond meal, chili powder, dried parsley, salt, and a pinch of black pepper. Mix well.

Beat the egg in a bowl, then stir in the mayo.

Slice the fish fillets into 1 inch by 2 inch strips. Coat in the egg mixture, then dredge in the cheese and almond meal mixture. Set aside.

Place a cast iron skillet over medium high flame and add about a half inch of coconut oil. Reduce to medium flame and heat through, then add the fish and cook for 2 minutes per side, or until golden brown and completely cooked.

Drain on a plate lined with paper towels, then arrange on a serving dish. Spoon the sauce into a dipping bowl, then serve.

Beef Chili

Makes 3 servings

Ingredients:
- 1 lb lean organic ground beef
- 1 quart bone or beef stock, low sodium
- ¼ cup olive oil
- 2 Tbsp ground flaxseeds
- 1/3 cup minced yellow onion
- 1 Tbsp chili powder
- 1 tsp dried oregano
- ½ tsp ground cumin
- ¼ tsp garlic powder
- Sea salt
- Freshly ground black pepper

Procedure:
Place a stockpot over high flame and heat through. Stir in the ground beef, then add the chili powder, cumin, garlic powder, and onion.

Sauté until the beef is browned and crumbly, then stir in the olive oil, beef broth, and ground flaxseeds. Bring the mixture to a boil.

Once boiling, reduce to a simmer over medium high flame. Simmer, uncovered, for about 30 minutes to an hour or until the chili is thickened.

Season to taste with salt and pepper and serve piping hot. If desired, store the beef chili in the refrigerator and reheat the following day.

Caribbean Chicken Stew

Makes 4 servings

Ingredients:
- 2 ½ lb chopped chicken pieces
- ½ quart chicken stock, low sodium
- 1 carrot, peeled and sliced
- ¾ cup cubed pumpkin
- ¾ cup cubed rutabaga
- ½ small turnip, cubed
- ½ cup chopped cauliflower florets
- 1 ½ cups shredded cabbage
- ½ tsp Tabasco sauce

For the marinade:
- 2 Tbsp freshly squeezed lime juice
- ¾ cup diced celery

- 1 small onion, minced
- 1 small ripe green bell pepper, seeded and chopped
- ½ Tbsp ground cumin
- ¼ tsp chicken bouillon granules
- ¼ tsp ground nutmeg

Procedure:

Combine all the ingredients for the marinade in a food processor and blend until smooth. Pour into a large bowl and add the chicken pieces. Turn several times to coat.

Cover the bowl and refrigerate to marinate the chicken for 8 hours, or overnight.

To cook, pour the chicken stock into the pot with the chicken pieces and marinade. Place over high flame and bring to a boil.

Once boiling, reduce to a simmer over low flame. Cover and simmer for 45 minutes to an hour, or until the chicken is cooked through.

Remove the chicken pieces from the pot and transfer to a plate. Strain the broth and discard any solids.

Pour the strained broth back into the pot and place over medium flame. Add the pumpkin, turnip, rutabaga and carrot, then simmer for 20 minutes.

Meanwhile, remove the bones from the chicken pieces, then stir into the pot. Mix everything well, then add the cauliflower and cabbage. Simmer for 20 minutes, then serve.

Side Dish Recipes

Buttered Spinach with Shallots and Bacon

Makes 3 servings

Ingredients:
- 8 oz spinach
- ¼ lb unprocessed bacon
- ¼ cup chopped shallots
- ¼ cup chopped white onion
- 1 Tbsp grass-fed butter

Procedure:
Dice the bacon and set aside.

Place a cast iron skillet over medium high flame and heat through. Once hot, add the bacon and sauté the bacon with the shallots and onion. Sauté for 12 minutes or until the onion is caramelized.

Reduce to medium flame, then stir in the spinach and sauté to combine. Cover the skillet and cook for 3 minutes or until the spinach is wilted.

Transfer to a serving plate, then serve right away.

Avocado and Cucumber Salad

Makes 4 servings

Ingredients:
- 1 cup diced English cucumber
- ½ cup diced avocado
- 1 small onion, diced
- 1 Tbsp freshly squeezed lime juice
- 1 Tbsp extra virgin olive oil
- Garlic powder
- Red pepper flakes
- Sea salt
- Freshly ground black pepper

Procedure:
Place the avocado in a bowl, then add the lime juice and toss gently to coat. Add the cucumber, onion, and olive oil, then toss again to coat.

Season to taste with salt, pepper, garlic powder, and red pepper flakes. Toss well, then cover and refrigerate until ready to serve.

Savory Roasted Spaghetti Squash with Kale

Makes 3 servings

Ingredients:
- Olive oil
- ½ spaghetti squash
- 2 cups chopped kale leaves
- 1 small onion, minced
- ½ tsp balsamic vinegar
- ¼ tsp chili powder
- Sea salt
- Freshly ground black pepper

Procedure:
Set the oven to 350 degrees F.

Scoop out the seeds and pulp from the spaghetti squash, then place it, exposed side facing upward, on the baking sheet. Brush with olive oil.

Bake the squash for 45 minutes to 1 hour, or until the squash is extra tender.

Meanwhile, place a skillet over medium high flame and heat through. Add half a tablespoon of olive oil, then sauté the onion until tender.

Stir in the kale and season with salt and pepper. Sauté until the kale is almost wilted and the onions are tender. Transfer to a plate and set aside.

Carefully remove the squash from the oven, then scrape out the roasted squash flesh using a fork. Transfer to a bowl.

Drizzle the balsamic vinegar and half a tablespoon of olive oil over the squash, then season to taste with chili powder, salt, and pepper.

Spread out the squash on a serving plate, then top with the kale and serve right away.

Buttered Mushrooms

Makes 3 servings

Ingredients:
- ½ lb fresh mushrooms (such as Portobello)
- 1 Tbsp grass-fed butter
- ½ tsp soy sauce, low sodium

Procedure:
Rinse the mushrooms, then set aside to drain.

Place a cast iron skillet over medium high flame and heat through. Once hot, add the butter, mushrooms, and soy sauce. Sauté until the mushrooms are tender and cooked through.

Transfer to a serving plate, then serve right away.

Mashed Zesty Garlic Cauliflower

Makes 2 servings

Ingredients:
- 2 cups chopped cauliflower florets
- 2 ½ Tbsp mayonnaise
- 1 small garlic clove, peeled
- ½ Tbsp water
- ½ Tbsp chopped fresh chives
- ¼ tsp freshly grated lime or lemon zest
- ¼ tsp sea salt
- Freshly ground black pepper

Procedure:

Combine the garlic, mayonnaise, and sea salt in a microwaveable bowl. Stir in the pinch of black pepper, then set aside.

Add the cauliflower and mix well to combine. Pour in the water, then microwave for 10 minutes, or until the cauliflower is extra tender.

Remove the cauliflower from the microwave and allow to cool completely. Once cooled, transfer to a food processor and add the chives, lemon juice, and zest. Blend until mashed.

Transfer to a serving bowl, then serve right away.

Cheesy Creamed Spinach
Makes 6 servings

Ingredients:
- 15 oz frozen spinach, thawed
- ¾ cup heavy cream
- 1/3 cup Parmesan cheese
- 3 Tbsp grass-fed butter
- Sea salt
- Freshly ground black pepper

- Ground nutmeg

Procedure:
Steam the spinach with a few tablespoons of water in the microwave until wilted. Drain thoroughly, then set aside.

In a saucepan, combine the spinach with the heavy cream, Parmesan cheese, and butter. Simmer over medium flame until cheese is melted. Stir well.

Season to taste with salt, pepper, and nutmeg, then transfer to a serving bowl. Serve right away.

Roasted Asparagus Wrapped in Bacon

Makes 6 servings

Ingredients:
- 2 Tbsp olive oil
- 1 lb asparagus, trimmed
- 6 slices unprocessed bacon
- 2 tsp minced garlic
- 1/3 cup mayonnaise
- 3 tsp freshly squeezed lemon juice
- Red chili flakes
- Sea salt
- Freshly ground black pepper

Procedure:

Set the oven to 400 degrees F. Line a baking sheet with aluminum foil, then set aside.

Divide the asparagus into 6 equal bundles. Wrap a slice of bacon around each bundle, then arrange on the prepared baking sheet.

Drizzle the olive oil over the asparagus bundle, then season with salt, pepper, and red chili flakes.

Bake for 25 minutes, or until the bacon is crisp and cooked through and the asparagus is browned and tender.

Meanwhile, combine the mayonnaise, garlic, lemon juice, and sea salt. Mix well.

Serve the asparagus with the dipping sauce.

Chapter 7 - One Week Meal Plan

The following one week keto meal plan is ideal for those who plan on preparing their meals every day. However, you can also plan on making your meals ahead of time and storing them in the refrigerator for easy reheating later on during the week. The 28 recipes in the previous chapters can be used to make several weeks' worth of meal plans and all you have to do is decide which ones to prep for each day.

Day 1
Breakfast: Herb and Mushroom Egg Scramble and/or Keto Espresso Smoothie
Lunch: (Main Dish) Baked Cheesy Chicken Balls, (Side Dish) Grilled Radicchio with Balsamic Vinaigrette
Dinner: (Main Dish) Poblano Peppers Stuffed with Pork and Cheese, (Side Dish) Buttered Spinach with Shallots and Bacon

Day 2
Breakfast: Coconut Banana Raisin Pancakes and/or Avocado and Raspberry Smoothie
Lunch: (Main Dish) Greek Tuna Salad, (Snack) Cheesy Broccoli

Dinner: (Main Dish) Sea Bass and Spinach with Coconut Lemon Sauce, (Side Dish) Avocado and Cucumber Salad

Day 3
Breakfast: Cheddar Flapjacks and/or Spiced Sweet Potato Smoothie
Lunch: (Main Dish) Chicken Barbecue Stew, (Side Dish) Cheddar Broccoli Biscuits
Dinner: (Main Dish) Stewed Beef and Mushrooms, (Side Dish) Savory Roasted Spaghetti Squash with Kale

Day 4
Breakfast: Bacon Avocado Breakfast Muffins and/or Green Blueberry Yogurt Smoothie
Lunch: (Main Dish) Avocado Beef Patties, (Side Dish) Mashed Cauliflower and Turnip
Dinner: (Main Dish) Cheesy Tuna and Cauliflower Casserole, (Side Dish) Buttered Mushrooms

Day 5
Breakfast: Bacon Ricotta Breakfast Muffins and/or Coconut Spice Smoothie
Lunch: (Main Dish) Oriental Style Chicken Salad, (Snack) Baked Garlic Parmesan Cauliflower
Dinner: (Main Dish) Crusted Fish Fillets with Dilled Sauce, (Side Dish) Mashed Zesty Garlic Cauliflower

Day 6

Breakfast: Creamy Keto Porridge and/or Peanut Butter Smoothie

Lunch: (Main Dish) Pork and Mushroom Meatballs, (Side Dish) Basic Cauliflower Rice

Dinner: (Main Dish) Beef Chili, (Side Dish) Cheesy Creamed Spinach

Day 7

Breakfast: Double Cheese Waffles and/or Buttered Pumpkin Spice Latte

Lunch: (Main Dish) Tex Mex Turkey Salad, (Snack) Tomato, Olive and Mozzarella Salad

Dinner: (Main Dish) Caribbean Chicken Stew, (Side Dish) Roasted Asparagus Wrapped in Bacon

In this one week meal plan, it is also assumed that you will be working out on a regular basis. Doing so will boost your metabolism and trigger your body to burn up your fat stores. On the other hand, if you will not be working out as frequently, then it is advised that you should reduce your portions for each meal from a quarter to half the recommended serving size.

Regardless of whether you are working out or not, you should stay hydrated by drinking lots of water. You should also snack on low carbohydrate vegetables to nourish your body with a variety of vitamins, minerals and other nutrients that it needs.

Conclusion

I hope this book was able to help you to start the keto diet and prepare delicious keto meals efficiently.

The next step is to create sustainable meal plans that will guide you while you are on the keto diet. Continue to stock up on keto foods and find ways to purchase organic ingredients from inexpensive and easily accessible sources. Finally, do not forget to exercise regularly so that you can achieve your health goals effectively.

What to read next

There are millions of books on Amazon. I'm are glad that you discovered my book and got to the end. Thank you for that.

I know the feeling after finishing a good book. The feeling of wanting more.

If you want more, check out my book on weight loss and training, *Intermittent Fasting: Wear Your Favorite Pair of Jeans, Look Good In Photos and Feel Sexy Again!*

Best,
Sebastian Beach